THE FOURTH
WHITE GOWN

THE FOURTH WHITE GOWN

IRMA O'CONOR PEPPER

St. Helena Press

Published by Gatekeeper Press
3971 Hoover Rd. Suite 77
Columbus, OH 43123-2839

ISBN: 9781619845688
eISBN: 9781619845695

Printed in the United States of America

CONTENTS

PREFACE

M Y MOTHER WROTE this book a half century ago. However, I only became aware of it last year when my wife, Francie, discovered it in one of those old dusty boxes that get stored away in an attic. I am so glad she found it.

The book tells the story of how my mother worked courageously and largely alone with my sister, Elizabeth, to overcome her addiction to pain-relieving drugs. My mother fictionalized the story by changing the names of the characters and compressing the challenges she and Elizabeth faced into a period of less than 24 hours. However, the reality of my mother's and sister's journey, filled with tragedy, courage and hope, is truthfully and vividly told.

The scourge of drug addiction is far broader today than it was fifty years ago.

My hope in publishing this book is that my mother's and sister's story will not only sensitize us to the devastating impact of drug addiction on the lives of both those addicted and those caring for them, but will encourage others close to the situation to do all they can to be of help.

—John Pepper
Former CEO and Chairman of
The Procter & Gamble Company

CHAPTER 1

To FEEL LIKE a dead weight is perhaps one of the best descriptions of utter exhaustion I know. And that was the way I felt. Oh, that my eyes would never have to open again; that my limbs would remain limp and still forever. Every nerve and muscle was crying for rest . . . rest . . . peaceful rest. But as always when exhausted, my eyes seemed to be forced open, the way they pried themselves open after the alarm clock went off in the early morning.

However, this was a Saturday. There would be no alarm clock today. My eyes didn't need to open; they could remain closed. What was the matter? The sunlight was pouring in through the windows. There were no drapes in the room and my eyelids could not take their place. I couldn't sleep any more. The sun had won, and my weariness had lost. Slowly I threw off the covers.

Sitting on the side of the bed, I looked around my bedroom. It was comparatively strange and empty, much like the rest of the new apartment I had recently taken, still without rugs or curtains, as it would undoubtedly remain for some time to come. The apartment could have been most attractive had I only possessed the money to decorate it even in simple taste. The two bedrooms, bath, living room with dining nook, and kitchen were roomy enough, and by long odds the most for the money anywhere in this section of the suburbs.

My eyes centered on the air conditioner which protruded from one of the bedroom walls. I couldn't help thinking how much comfort new conveniences gave today, but how superficial they were by comparison to the pleasure of happy, loving affection and companionship.

Mine was a loneliness which came of desperation. Not that I didn't have friends. I was blessed with many. They could help in some ways, but my troubles were of such a deep nature only my own family could have provided the continuing and sustained support necessary to resolve them. And there was no one of my own nearby; I had to walk alone.

The very help I knew my daughter required was the most formidable for me to provide. It was help I knew must be given, but in giving it, I myself also needed aid and assistance so desperately.

I must get up. The day might be long and perhaps difficult. This I knew all too well. Looking around, I saw the two windows, bare without curtains or drapes, the pair of bureaus, lovely enough in themselves, but without any of my touches of boudoir charm. I hadn't even managed to have the large maple mirror hung yet. It was almost impossible to accomplish even the little required chores at home when I worked every day except Saturday.

Slipping into my bedroom slippers and bathrobe, I wearily struggled into the bathroom and began to brush my teeth. The telephone rang.

"Hi, Mother."

"Shirley. This is a surprise, so early."

"I have permission to come home for the day—really until tomorrow if you'll let me."

We were off again. What should I answer? And why hadn't

the doctors called me first so I could have discussed Shirley's condition with them?

It wasn't a question of my not wanting to take Shirley for the day. It was a question of my own capabilities. Sometimes I wondered if she didn't ask the doctors if she could come home, only to have them say, "Ask your mother." In this way, the responsibility for the decision was shifted to someone else's shoulders.

I found myself answering Shirley in the same nervous undertones I had so often been accused of by her and her doctors.

"Did the doctors say it was all right, Shirley?"

"Of course they did. I can come home anytime you'll let me. I thought I told you that the other day."

Underneath I was really frightened. If only I had had an opportunity to talk to them before she called. Shirley undoubtedly thought I was a little nervous, but believe me, I was filled with sincere apprehension and fear.

My daughter Shirley was a beautiful girl and a patient in a State Hospital, the most recent hospital of many. She had a most attractive turned-up nose, a fair complexion (the type of skin which sunburns easily), and she would have been a light brown-haired lassie if she hadn't insisted lately on bleaching her hair to a point where it was almost a yellowish orange color. Shirley was a larger girl in frame than I, taller and about ten pounds heavier.

In short, she was a modern girl. Men turned and stared at her when she walked by. Then their eyes inevitably turned to her legs, especially the right leg. And maybe this was the source of all of Shirley's troubles, at least an awful lot of them. You see, Shirley had a fused right knee. She had originally hurt her leg in an automobile accident, and had had many operations on the leg. She had suffered much pain during these past several years due to the almost never-ending surgery, which resulted in multitudinous medical complications and critical infections. Anyway, one of the net results was a fusion, a right leg which never would be bent again. I suppose she thought this made her unattractive, but it wasn't true. Maybe this was her basic problem. Who knew? Certainly no psychiatrist had made any real progress to date.

There was one more thing you should know about Shirley. She conned anyone. I mean she could convince anyone about anything. She was always believed, and this seemed to be true regardless of any facts to the contrary. Shirley didn't only fool the amateurs; she fooled the professionals, the doctors. And not only the general practitioners, orthopedists, or surgeons, but the psychiatrists themselves. Why, I remembered the time Shirley had been taken to the hospital in a strait jacket. She'd been on a real binge for days and was in a most rebellious mood, completely antagonistic towards everyone. Yet, having been taken to the hospital under these conditions, unbelievably she was allowed to come home the very next weekend. Yes—it was unbelievable—unbelievable unless you knew Shirley.

"What time do you want me to pick you up, Shirley?"

"Eight thirty would be fine, Mother."

"Eight thirty?"

"Yes, Mother."

"Why, Shirley, it's eight o'clock now. I can't possibly be over there by eight thirty, dear. It will be closer to nine thirty."

"All right, Mother. I'll be waiting by the front door of the main building. See you! Good-bye."

Well, I knew I would have to scramble. That was another important characteristic of Shirley's. We should have baptized her with the middle name of Persistence. No one gave Shirley "no" for an answer. You might say "no" to her once, but if it was something she really wanted, she would try again and again until the "no" became an erased answer. Either that or she would maneuver events in such a way as to make the desired results accomplished facts.

I had to tear now. Into the kitchen to put the percolator on and to pour a glass of orange juice; back to the bedroom to get my vitamin pill; then into the bathroom to start my bath water, and back to the kitchen to take the pill and drink my orange juice. At last I was ready to check the bath water, and slipped into the tub. The water felt good, and I relaxed momentarily. And the soap was scented. I had purchased it only yesterday. Another five minutes and I would be out of the tub and getting dressed.

"Dang, that telephone again."

Sometimes I wanted to rip the phone out of the wall, but it was a very real comfort to know I had one since I was alone. The night could be long, indeed, without a telephone.

Well, up and out of the tub, a hasty drying with the big towel, and I was back in the bedroom grabbing the telephone.

"Hello."

"Mrs. Daniels?"

"Yes."

"This is Mr. Eastman of the Dorf Delicatessen. We are the approved dealers for the Arms Apartments in regard to delivering the daily newspapers. Would you care to receive the Kingstown morning paper each day?"

"Well, Mr. Eastman, I'm very busy now. Could you call me sometime this afternoon?"

"Certainly, Mrs. Daniels. I'm sorry if I disturbed you. Would three o'clock be alright?"

"Three o'clock would be fine, Mr. Eastman. Thank you for calling."

Now why had I bothered to answer the telephone? And

why couldn't I have told him abruptly and immediately that I didn't want the paper? Why did I always have to be so polite, such a lady? Well, it was too late to act otherwise now.

What to wear? Perhaps the green wool dress with the black shoes. Now where had I put that dress? Everything was in the wrong place—not really the wrong place, since I had so recently moved into the apartment, but certainly things were not in the orderly placement I had hoped for by now. I looked in another closet. There was the dress, thank heavens. It was now ten after nine. Shirley would be angry. I wouldn't even have time to toast an English muffin. I was determined to have my coffee, though, if I had to drink it while I was getting dressed.

My new apartment was on the second floor. I went down two or three steps, then ran back to be sure I'd locked the door. On down the stairs again to the only possession I thoroughly enjoyed—my new car. It gave me a freedom of movement, and I did like the power steering. Where had I put those keys? My purse looked awful. I should clean it out, but I had to hurry or I would be in real trouble with Shirley. Please God, had I lost the keys? Maybe I'd left them back at the apartment, but they should be here. They had to be in my purse. Another look. Ah, there they were.

Fortunately, the car was new and started immediately. I looked at myself in the mirror. It was a worried tired face that stared back at me. I could have used more lipstick. Actually, I never used any other make-up except lipstick. Perhaps today was a day for considerably more make-up.

The time was then nine thirty. I was already late, and it would take a good half an hour to reach the hospital. My apartment was situated on the highest hill of the new complex of buildings. As I drove down the hill, I thought how pleasant it was to be up so high. There was a "stop" sign at the bottom of the incline, after which I had to turn to the right in order to get out on the main road. It was one of my little pleasures to go right through the "stop" sign. No law was being broken however, since the new road was not yet finished.

I was out on the highway at last, and suddenly noticed the gas tank was almost empty. Fortunately, there was a gas station on my way, and I turned in, relieved to have made it in time.

"Two dollars' worth of regular, and will you check the oil and water, please? And do you have a pay phone inside?"

"Yes, ma'am, we do."

"Thank-you."

I would have to call Shirley and tell her I was going to be late. It took a few minutes for the switchboard operator to get her to the phone at the hospital.

"Shirley. This is Mother."

"Hi. Did you have an accident?"

"No. Some salesman called, and I just couldn't get away, but I'll be there shortly now. All right?"

"All right. Good-bye."

Well, thank goodness, she sounded pleasant, and not a bit angry. The salesman story was certainly an exaggeration, but I couldn't have made it any faster, regardless. Back in the car, I hoped desperately I'd been right about Shirley's mood on the phone. I could have no real assurance, because as I've said, Shirley could fool anyone. There might have been another patient near the telephone at the hospital—someone she was afraid could overhear her conversation. Shirley could be as sweet as pie one minute to a stranger. When the stranger left, her conversation could be viciously critical, particularly if she hadn't liked him. Some of the words she had acquired in her vocabulary I had never heard before, but anyone would have recognized they were sordid and dirty, partly from her intonation. When Shirley wasn't well, a visitor knew very quickly when his status in our home was no longer that of a guest.

This was the tragedy about the whole case. Shirley had been such a thoroughly fine girl—charm, personality, poise, a composite of everything that constituted an attractive young woman. She possessed all those attributes associated with a girl who was well-educated, and who was accustomed to being with people who place their values in life on integrity and honesty. She had so much to offer; an infectious laugh, a natural athletic ability, a good dancer. But all this was seven years ago, and I had reached a point where it was difficult for me to remember the way things were prior to her knee injury. If Shirley were only sixteen again. It didn't take very long to change a person. How differently I would have done things had I been able to go back. A totally different path would have been followed in Shirley's case.

You live for your children. Would she ever be well again? Could she ever snap out of it? Dozens of questions passed through my mind, almost simultaneously. And they would always be there until and unless a cure was discovered. I wondered, too, about the few people I knew who had connived and cheated their ways through life. Their families seemed to enjoy good health; there were no apparent difficulties. The balancing of the books certainly didn't seem to be correct, particularly when I'd tried in every possible way to make things go right. Life was easy to accept when you were well and happy, and not burdened with deep trouble and tragedy.

Shirley's injury had occurred about seven years ago, and it was nearly four years ago when she had started to exhibit decided abnormalities in addition to her physical problems. Exactly where the line should be drawn between the physical and mental was a difficult question for anyone to determine.

At first it was impossible to figure out the reasons for the abnormalities and I tried to pass them off. Then began the lies—or were they the truths? There was one conclusion I had reached concerning this question. Every person thought that he or she was clever, at least in some way. I think I'm clever; you think you're clever. Someone tells you something factual, a most plausible story—at least it sounds factual and plausible. Yet you know from experience this particular person always exaggerates. However, since you are clever, you consider yourself capable of discerning the amount of exaggeration involved. It doesn't occur to you that everything related is completely false, or that it has been turned around one hundred and eighty degrees. When you've been fooled often enough, then you become apprehensive about your own ability to discern and determine truth. At least this is what happened to me. What was a lie? What part was truth? I had decided I never really knew, and I'd ceased trying to figure it out.

I was driving too fast. I suddenly realized it in the midst of my thoughts. I was on Hillside Road now, going toward Victory Highway. At the dead-end intersection, I turned right and drove the mile to the entrance to the State Hospital. The sweeping drive leading into the grounds had been built between two fieldstone columns. This didn't mean the hospital was old. In fact, it was very new, built about five years ago, boasting the most modern facilities for institutions of this type. I understood the hospital would not accept any more patients at this time even though several of their buildings were not occupied. The Staff's policy, honest and proper, was to ensure the optimum ratio of personnel to patients.

I had reached the entrance to the hospital. A car was coming toward me, and since I had to make a left-hand turn,

I waited until it passed. With the blinker light flashing a warning signal to the traffic behind me, I at last turned into the drive off Victory Highway, resolutely determined to make the day a success in every way.

The Admissions Building at the hospital was six stories high with a big esplanade in front, and a cantilever roof projection over the walk. The roof itself was shaped in an arc as if cut from a large circle. It was supported by several stainless steel columns which were shiny, but shiny in the manner of St. Paul's, "I see now, as in a dark mirror."

On the fifth and sixth floors were the wards for the sickest patients, the severest cases, those who had tried to commit suicide or who had been violent. Beyond the Main Building were several one-story modern institutional units, shaped in a ladder design, so that each structure was separate, but still connected, thus obviating exposure during inclement weather. The patients who resided in these buildings had shown definite recuperative progress and sufficient emotional stability to be granted certain freedom of movement and ground privileges.

Opposite Admissions was the recreational hall and auditorium, commonly referred to by the patients as RT, for recreational therapy. Bowling alleys, a swimming pool, snack bar, movie theatre and squash courts made up RT.

I drove into the visitor's parking lot and began to search for an empty space. The first row was full. Suddenly I spotted an opening, but as luck would have it, when I arrived I saw it was already occupied by a small foreign car. Finally, I ended up in the last row, the farthest distance from where I was to meet Shirley.

This was the moment when I always got nervous. The place, lovely as it looked with its beautiful trees and landscaping, gave me chills. It wasn't because of the patients in general, but rather that my daughter was here. No one, particularly I, ever thought this could happen. But it had.

Now it was no longer the case that illness had struck someone else. It had become my own problem in my own family. I remembered the little girl who lived two doors away from us many years ago; the little girl who came over to our house and called, "Hey, Shirley; hey, Shirley," with me remonstrating, "Joannie. You should ring the doorbell when you want Shirley to come out and play with you."

Then it had been a sick little girl and her parents who were very upset. When I saw Joannie's mother and father, I remembered saying, "Now, Mrs. Sillman, please try not to worry too much. They have made such wonderful progress in treating patients within the past twenty years. I'm sure Joannie will be all right soon, and I will say a prayer for both of you."

I would leave them thinking I'd comforted them; sincerely believing that I'd been a source of real consolation and strength. Now I knew and understood Mrs. Sillman's anguish as I couldn't before. I also knew I hadn't helped her.

Please God, don't let Shirley be cross and irritable today. Entering the Admissions Building was like walking into a hotel lobby. I took a deep breath and held onto my purse tightly so that my hands would not shake so much.

I was thankful Shirley would be waiting on the main floor and not upstairs. I always panicked when I had to use one of the elevators. It was a complicated procedure. A key was necessary both to call the elevator and to designate the floor desired. An attendant always did this for me, then stepped out quickly and I was on my way alone. I was always afraid the elevator might stop, or worse, as sometimes happened, that a patient would be my only companion on the ride.

Shirley wasn't there. I wondered whether something had happened and inquired at the Information Desk.

"Yes?"

"My daughter, Shirley Daniels, was supposed to meet me here in the lobby. Have you seen her, or could you find out where she might be?"

"Yes, Mrs. Daniels. Shirley was here just a second ago; she's been waiting for you. Maybe she stepped into the Ladies Room."

"Thank you. I'll look around."

There she was, coming out of the phone booth. She'd probably been trying to reach me at home.

"Shirley!"

I hoped my voice wasn't that high nervous one, the one I seemed to reserve for these occasions. We started to move towards each other. I gave her a kiss.

"You look lovely, Shirley." And she did.

"Mother, I was getting worried. I thought you might have had an accident." She said this laughingly, so I knew we would have a nice beginning.

"Here. Let me carry your suitcase." I reached for her bag.

"No, thank you. I can manage both it and my dresses. Why don't you go ahead and bring the car to the front entrance?"

"Good idea. I'm parked at the far end of the lot."

As I went out the door, I could get a panoramic view of the entire parking area. Being Saturday, there were many cars. People were carrying suitcases, and getting into automobiles to go home for a night. Each car had one patient. Everyone was smiling, looking cheerful, but underneath, in each person's heart, I knew, there was a sense of fear. Would this weekend work out? Would the police have to be called?

As we drove way I noticed how attractive Shirley was. A very beautiful girl. Tragic was the only word which described her situation. Her progress and eventual release from the institution, as opposed to a permanent commitment, resided within herself. Others might aid her, but in the final analysis it would be Shirley alone who would determine the years to come.

You see, my daughter Shirley was a dope addict. She was a victim of the medical era in which she lived. She didn't use a needle; it was more refined than that. She took pills, all kinds of pills—tranquilizers, sleeping pills, depressants, anti-depressants. Her rate of consumption was enormous. For a long time, I'd wondered how anyone could obtain so much medication. However, after I had lived with the problem, I learned how easily pills were acquired. It was so simple, in fact, that it was small wonder I had been misled for so many years.

All addicts are very clever. Once, while emptying a waste basket, I found an empty prescription bottle. To my astonishment, the label indicated the prescription had been made out in Shirley's name, and my own doctor was listed as the prescribing physician. Thoroughly shaken, I drove to his office and demanded an explanation.

Very calmly, he dialed the drug store in question, and ascertained all the details. After assuring me that he had never seen nor talked to Shirley in his life, he explained what had happened. Under existing drug regulations, a doctor may prescribe once by telephone. A telephoned prescription, however, may only be refilled by written order. Shirley must have had a male accomplice impersonate my doctor, on this particular occasion. However, there were numerous drug stores and physicians in the area. How many times this impersonation had taken place no one would ever know.

The money? How had she paid for the pills?

"Did I have seven or twelve dollars in my wallet?"

I would miss small amounts from time to time, and of course would never receive any change when Shirley returned from the store. Bills from both doctors and pharmacies must have poured in, although I was never aware of them until the collection agencies began to call me at my office. Every piece of mail was censored by Shirley. Since the inception of her addiction, I had never opened a letter of my own. Even when we both arrived home together, regardless of my protestations, she took charge of all the mail. Why had I allowed this? It was far easier than having a vehement argument, or even worse, being physically attacked for supposedly false accusations.

Now you know Shirley's problem, and therefore my problem. It all might not have happened if, as I said before, Shirley had not been the victim of the medical world in which she lived. So many, many operations, countless antibiotics and drugs to save her life from infections. It had been a nightmare, particularly the involvement with the pills and medications given to relieve her incessant pain and anxiety.

"Did you have a nice week, Shirley?"

"Pretty good, but it's certainly better to be out."

"Try not to think about it, dear. We'll have a good time today. Perhaps our first stop should be at the market; we don't have much of a supply of groceries at home."

"Whatever you say, Mother. Anything will be fine with me."

"I think we might splurge a bit today and eat lunch out rather than at home, so we won't include that meal in the order."

"Has Jim called at all this week, Mother?"

"Yes. He seems to be doing fine. Although I miss him very much, as you do, I'm glad his job has taken him out of town. I think he has a better chance there."

"Yes, I suppose so. But we do need a man in the family so very much."

Jim was my son, and Shirley's brother, a very mature young man who had recently started a job in Gary, Indiana. It had been the best solution all the way around, although the final wrench of parting with him had been a rugged one. Most of all, it was best for Jim. He usually called me once a week. The main subject, of course, was Shirley. How was she doing? What were her chances of recovery?

It had been my suggestion that Jim should work in Indiana. Had he remained here, he would have had little chance of success. With Shirley in and out of the hospital, any regular or normal life was impossible. To live with a drug addict was completely exhausting and debilitating. It had never made sense to me that everyone should be destroyed by association, and since Jim would have the best possible chance in life, he should have it. A fine opportunity had presented itself, and I insisted he take it.

Well, here we were at the market, and our day was one-half hour long. So far so good. The first test was coming. If I remained in the market too long, she might get nervous or restless.

"Shirley, what would you especially like for the weekend?"

"Really, Mother, I don't care. Anything would taste good after institutional cooking. I get so tired of some of the meals. The worst aspect, though, is the complete lack of table manners. It's all I can do to stay at the table sometimes."

"Well, why don't you take five dollars and get something you might enjoy; some things you can take back with you?"

"Thank you. You know, Mother, you're wonderful."

I gave Shirley the money and she moved off and began to look at the various displays. I pushed my cart around, gathering the groceries needed for the weekend. By the time I'd reached the next to last aisle of groceries and was about to go over to the produce stand, Shirley approached with her arms filled with food. Her supply for the hospital looked ample, and most important, there was no sign of any irritation on her face; she looked very pleased and completely relaxed.

We finished shopping, and called a grocery boy to take our packages out to the car, got in and prepared to leave the parking lot. I, of course, was driving because Shirley was not allowed to drive. Not that she still didn't have a valid license. She never did lose it officially. But she was very much afraid to take the wheel now. Before, she would often use the car surreptitiously when she was under the influence of drugs. I was always dreadfully afraid she might run down some poor child, but this reasoning never made much of an impression on her at the time. However, when I warned her she would be subject to a jail sentence if the police ever stopped her while she was under the influence of drugs, this had some effect.

"Where would you like to have lunch, dear? Shall we go over to Parodi's? They have fine Italian food and you love spaghetti."

"No, Mother, unless you want to, of course. Why not the Scandinavian? We haven't been there for ages."

"That would be fun, Shirley. And they do have a grand smorgasbord; the Swedish meatballs are out of this world."

It took about fifteen minutes to reach the Scandinavian. This, plus the hour spent at the market placed the time at twelve-thirty in the afternoon. We had already been two hours together, and it was quite like the old days again. Maybe there had been a change for the better, at last.

"Yes? How many will there be in your party, Madame?"

"Only two of us, thank you."

There were not many people at the Scandinavian as it was a Saturday, and the normally heavy crowd of businessmen were not here today. Shirley and I were led to a nice quiet table by the window. This was a place I always enjoyed; there was enough light to see each other, I suppose because people had to see the smorgasbord. As we sat down, however, Shirley gave a short disappointed sigh.

"Oh, there's no smorgasbord today, Mother. See the notice on the table."

"I'm sorry, Shirley. I'm sure, though, they have some very good luncheons on the regular menu."

In a few minutes our waiter returned.

"May I take your order now, ladies, or would you like to have a cocktail before luncheon?"

"We'll order now, thank you. What have you decided to have, Shirley?"

"I'll have a cup of clam chowder first, please; then spaghetti with Swedish meatballs, lima beans, and salad with Russian dressing."

"Just a club sandwich on toast for me, thank you, and a cup of coffee."

As the waiter left, we looked into each others' eyes and both of us began to smile at the same time.

"How have you been, Shirley?" I asked for the twentieth time, and impulsively reached over and took her hand. When I did my eyes began to well up with tears.

I struggled for control and began to talk about clothes, shoes, and the various accessories both our wardrobes lacked desperately at the moment. We decided a trip to a department store would be very much in order before we went home. It would be fun to look, even if we didn't buy anything.

Shirley talked and we both began to relax. She commenced by relating some stories about various patients at the hospital, some of whom I had met. Many of the incidents were very funny, and Shirley narrated them with a genuine sense of humor. We both had the same infectious laugh, and became almost loud on occasion. It seemed a very healthy sign that

Shirley could laugh about her surroundings and the abnormal events inevitably connected with them.

When she told me about her possible new job at the Hospital, we both became hysterical. At the State Hospital, when a patient becomes somewhat quiet and generally improved, he was usually assigned to physical or occupational therapy. Positions requiring definite responsibility were often assigned to those who had the requisite talents. Shirley's potential position, believe it or not, was secretary in the pharmaceutical department. Because the present atmosphere was not a moody one, I was able to comment laughingly that it was rather like giving an alcoholic a job as a bartender.

Shirley answered with a smile. "It certainly is, inasmuch as I could have access to all the drawers containing sample medications. They would be easy to take, I imagine."

I wondered about the plausibility of this therapy myself.

"Can you understand their considering me? They mustn't know what I'm doing in the hospital, or why I'm there."

I was thrilled with this piece of news now that I had had a few minutes to think it over. It must be a very good sign. The doctors would not be so stupid as to have a girl with Shirley's problem work around her greatest temptation. She was evidently making progress.

The waiter came over and asked if we wanted dessert. Shirley ordered pie a la mode, and I had another cup of coffee.

Leaving the Scandinavian parking lot was a chore. We had to go through a stop sign, cross to the other side of the highway, and turn left. Because of heavy traffic it took us five minutes to make the turn. Normally, this would be a period of restraint and little or no talking, but due to the genuine fun we'd had at lunch, we sat and made small talk about the purchases we would have liked to make at the department store.

There was certainly a big question as to whether we could buy anything at the store. My checking account was very low. However, if it had contained all my resources today, I might have spent everything, since hope was once again beating in step with my heart. We decided that we would each buy stockings, and Shirley a pair of shoes; also we would walk around the store to look at anything new that might have been added to the "Fashion Parade" recently. Both of us were completely out of step and contact with fashion's fancy, and had no idea what the stylists were inveigling buyers to purchase this year.

We went to a suburban branch of a leading city department store. The prices were a little higher than some of the other stores, and I had often felt their "sales" were not really "sales." But it was convenient and attractive, always the right temperature, winter or summer, and was never crowded.

After purchasing our stockings, Shirley looked at a new pair of shoes, while I sauntered over to admire the beautiful lingerie displayed on the models. Shirley usually wore out her shoes faster than other people. I should say one shoe, due to her fused knee. The other one was always in excellent shape by comparison.

I purchased a few small items at the notions counter and wandered back toward the shoe salon. Shirley had evidently made her selection and left. She wasn't there. I looked around the store, and with relief I spotted her over at the cosmetics counter.

Coming up quietly behind her, I tapped her on the shoulder and said, "Boo."

She turned, startled, and we both laughed at the draculean mother I pretended to be. "Did you want something else, Shirley?"

"Yes. I'd love some spray cologne. I did buy some shoes,

though they're not exactly what I was looking for. But they're practical and will be comfortable to wear around the grounds and at my new job."

Together we looked at coats and a few dresses, in particular some beautiful cocktail dresses. Almost simultaneously we turned away, and began a casual walk to the car. It was about a quarter to three, and it would be a good half to three-quarters of an hour before we could possibly reach home.

A great deal of construction work was still in progress at the apartment compound as we drove in the main driveway. Although it was a Saturday, men were busy planting shrubbery and trying to clean up the grounds. There was plenty of parking space in front of our apartment unit, because one young married couple and I were the only occupants so far in the eight-apartment building.

Fortunately, the entrance to their apartment faced ours and I could at least hear an occasional friendly movement at night. It was comforting since I lived alone.

Due to our purchases and Shirley's suitcase and dresses, three trips were necessary before we succeeded in emptying the car. Shirley jokingly offered to carry my purse up to the apartment on the last trip, which I allowed her to do.

At last the final package was deposited on the kitchen counter and I was relieved that things were going so well. Entering my apartment from the hall it was a direct step into the living room. There was no foyer or vestibule. To the left of the entrance door was the front wall, and to the right the living room, 19 feet by 10. A small corridor led from the rear wall of the living room into the den, really another bedroom and about the same width as the living room. Off the corridor to the right was a full bath, and to the left was the master bedroom. This comprised the right half of the apartment.

Directly across from the entrance door was the dining area, in the middle of which was a small drop-leaf cherry table. No partition divided this area from the living room. A door on the right led to the kitchen which extended back about 10 feet toward the rear of the apartment. The far wall of the kitchen abutted the large bedroom.

We immediately engaged ourselves with various activities. I picked up things in the den and then made up the beds with fresh linens. Shirley helped me after she had unpacked. We then went out to the kitchen to unpack the groceries. Having Shirley there was a great help since she was a good two inches taller than I, and could reach the top shelves easily.

The telephone rang.

"I'll answer it, Shirley. You take it easy now."

I hurried to the den.

"Mrs. Daniels. This is Mr. Eastman of the Dorf Delicatessen calling again about the daily paper."

"Oh, yes, Mr. Eastman. I'm sorry I wasn't in at three. I was delayed. I'd like to begin taking the paper."

"Fine, Mrs. Daniels. We'll begin tomorrow morning. Thank you very much."

"Who was that, Mother?" Shirley called.

"Oh, a Mr. Eastman calling me about subscribing to the daily paper."

I returned to the kitchen. Shirley had turned on the radio when we first came home so that most of the surface noises were muffled. During the unpacking and general straightening up, we had maintained our mood of convivial conversation and good humor.

All of a sudden, however, I noticed that Shirley had left the kitchen. Nor was she in the living room. Almost at the same moment, I heard the noise—a loud click.

CHAPTER 2

I T WAS LIKE a rifle shot going off in the very room where I was standing. Loud . . . so loud that my ears were deafened and I wanted to scream and scream and scream.

What was this noise, this click, that was almost like an explosion to me? Nothing more than the sound of the locking of the bathroom door, not an unusual sound in itself, but to me a frightening indication that Shirley might be taking medication.

It had been her pattern for many years to take pills surreptitiously behind the locked bathroom door. My alertness was understandable and very like that subconscious sense that never allows a mother to go completely to sleep until she knows her children have come home at night.

Maybe I was overly suspicious today. Maybe it was just force of habit that had caused Shirley to lock the door, habit formed both at home and in the State Hospital. I decided to try the bathroom door, hoping perhaps I might have been mistaken. It was locked.

I was beginning to feel apprehensive. I had to admit it, though hoping all along I was wrong. In a few minutes Shirley came out of the bathroom and sat down in the living room. I attempted to submerge my suspicions and fears, but they were vibrantly alert and watchful for any sign of disturbed action or change that might manifest itself in her behavior.

"You'll never know, Mother, how good it is to be home again, if only to set the table for dinner for you." And she really was sincere in this remark. Little things to do about the house always had and still did mean a great deal to Shirley. She commented on the attractiveness of the apartment, and the great possibilities it offered for doing an excellent decorating job, money permitting. She also remarked on the relative peace and quiet compared to the hospital.

Peaceful it might have seemed, but if a fluoroscope had been handy, my stomach would have shown at least one square knot per inch of the picture. For suddenly, dreadfully, my hopes had vanished. That old nagging feeling of dread began—that feeling of dread I had experienced so often, which was like a furious crescendo in music, ever building up and increasing in intensity. It emanated from an inner intuitive sense that to all outward appearances at this stage was neither obvious nor perceptible. A mother usually knows her children. I prayed silently it wasn't true. It wasn't going to happen again.

It might have been I noticed a change in her eyes first, yet an outsider would have seen nothing wrong with them. Maybe she knew she had done something wrong, and felt subconsciously a signal must be given to those who loved her. Although I sensed the change strongly, and was encompassed with increasing waves of dread, still I didn't want to believe it.

Picking up a magazine, I pretended to busy myself reading, but never actually saw the pages of print. After about fifteen minutes Shirley suddenly announced, "I think I'll do some laundry now and set the table later."

Her speech had definitely changed, not in any way that a stranger might notice, but in the way so well known to me.

It had changed. Now I knew. It was like a blow to my solar plexus. No, not like a blow to my solar plexus; it was as if, without experiencing any pain, my stomach had been cut out with a very sharp knife. It was as if I had remained conscious after taking an anesthetic, watching someone cut me open and sew me up again without a trace of stitches.

I was in a void. I felt empty and temporarily paralyzed and speechless. I could only nod my head in agreement to her announcement. I couldn't move—couldn't even light a cigarette. I just sat and remained motionless for a time that would never be a part of my life, a time that had never been a part of it. Perhaps a serious accident had occurred during that time; perhaps a man and his wife had had an argument; maybe you could swear in court that you had been taking a nap during that period of emptiness. Those minutes may have made history for others, but for me they had never existed.

Slowly, very slowly, I came out of the timeless void and gradually became aware of events going on around me again. History picked itself up for me, and my memory again began recording events. It was about a quarter to four.

I realized she must have gone into the bedroom, taken some underwear, and returned to the bathroom. The water was running in the bathtub. I didn't say a word. I knew now. I could tell. I knew, knew the picture all too well.

She was washing underwear. I didn't know whether it was clean underwear or dirty underwear, or a mixture of the two.

From now on she would have to move. Nothing would be done in slow motion. It was a familiar mood, this heightening of activity—a familiar mood during which her activity would increase for some time to come.

I still wasn't sure if I could move, but thought I might be able to get to the kitchen, robot-like. The sound of the water pouring into the bathtub was like the roar of Niagara Falls in my ears. I made it out to the kitchen and put water on for a cup of tea. Waiting for the water to boil, I leaned my head wearily against one of the cabinets, and when it was ready I drank it standing up rather than going in to the dining room table.

While drinking the tea, my mind began to race and my brain to think—think—think. I knew I had to consider various alternatives, but my thoughts were running too fast. I realized only too well that a solution must be found, but underneath I was afraid there was no solution. I only hoped she had taken a medication that would eventually induce sleep. Whatever she had taken, it must have been a heavy dose in order for it to act so fast.

Had I sat at the dining room table I would have been able to see the bathroom door, and to possibly catch a glimpse of Shirley. But I didn't want to see her. I didn't want to see my daughter incoherent, and with an almost maniacal face. I wanted to run—to run and escape.

There were two types of medication she might have taken. One would induce tiredness, loss of equilibrium, and eventually periods of sleep. The other type would also induce loss of equilibrium, but would make her hyperactive. Any form of activity performed under the influence of the latter type was performed with vigorous zest and motion.

Without exaggerating, I had seen Shirley go for periods of 72 hours on many occasions without sleeping or even lying down. Constant and primarily destructive activity constituted her actions during these periods.

At first, when these hyperactive binges occurred, I would follow her around trying to save various items from destruction—putting things away and in general attempting to clean up the damage as it happened. After several hours I would sit down wearily, listening for the next crash, gradually becoming numb to all that was happening. After the first 24 hours, I would try to get her to go to bed.

I would reason in this fashion. I was exhausted and ready to collapse. Therefore, Shirley should feel even more tired and would surely be prepared to rest. However, it was never any use, and I should have realized the hopelessness of trying. In the end, I would sit and watch her erratic movements around the apartment. Any endeavor to persuade her to sleep was like stopping a forest fire with a garden watering can.

Finally, I would doze myself, always afraid of something catastrophic occurring while my eyes were closed; afraid that she might not be there when I awoke; that somehow she might have found the keys and taken the car and become involved in an accident; or worse, that while smoking, she might have started a fire.

Sometimes, when I was lucky, I persuaded a doctor to come, and he would administer a sedative to knock her out. Most of the doctors in the earlier years had been completely taken in by her story that she was not taking anything. All kinds of diagnoses were given to explain her condition and behavior. It was true that she had an unbelievable medical history with every kind of complication and tragedy developing in the case of her bone disease and infection.

I finished the cup of tea and forced my feet towards the living room trying to compose my face. This was always most important, to have a strong, calm face; for a controlled exterior, even though forced, seemed to help in my thinking and prevented the loss of my emotional control. Also, if possible, my voice had to sound normal.

I became aware of water still running in the bathroom, but could hear no other sounds of movement in the apartment. Casually, I sauntered past the bathroom door. I had to be very careful to avoid arousing Shirley's suspicions. In no way could I permit her to suspect I knew she wasn't herself. I had decided to pretend I needed a handkerchief if she asked what I was doing. She would never really inquire where I was going. Rather, she would vehemently state, "What are you sneaking around for? Why don't you mind your own business?"

Shirley's method was to overcome her misdeeds by a vicious yelling denial that nothing was wrong with her.

As I came abreast of the bathroom door, I saw it was open. I looked in. She was not there but the water had reached the top of the bathtub and was beginning to overflow. I dashed in and turned it off. Underwear was both in the tub and on the wet floor. I grabbed some towels and wiped up most of the water.

The bedroom door was shut. Quietly I tiptoed over and listened but could hear nothing from within. Slowly I turned the doorknob and looked around. She appeared to be sound asleep on her bed. Noiselessly, I closed the door and returned to the living room, thinking desperately about what I had to do.

I had learned through bitter experience on more than one occasion it was hopeless to call the hospital. Being a weekend, there was little chance of finding her doctor there, and even if he had been, small hope of being able to speak with him. This, I believed, was a grave error, for Shirley's doctor had far greater control over her than I in her present condition, and might have had a chance to arrest any further progression at this time.

In any case, the only answer ever given under these circumstances was to call the police, a most unpleasant procedure, at best. The hospital authorities were firm on this subject.

As I mentioned previously, once it had taken four policemen to put Shirley in a strait jacket, with all the accompanying noise and notoriety. If there was any other way to handle the problem, I wished to do it that way, for I had found out through experience any other method was more expedient.

I finally decided to concentrate on putting things away she might knock over later on. With this in my mind, I had my beautiful karamus Madonna in my hands, and was placing it in a drawer when the phone rang. I ran to the phone, so anxious to talk to someone, to get some advice, to get some help. I knew that disaster was imminent.

"Hello."

"Mary, this is Ted. How have you been and may I talk to Shirley, please?"

Ted was my husband, and we had been separated for some time. He was worthless, and used Shirley as a subterfuge in order to speak to me. Suffice to explain, he had been an investment broker and the director of a bank at the age of thirty-one. Today he was a night clerk at a motel on the midnight to eight a.m. shift. Drinking and its debilitating effects had taken a large and costly toll on his life, and consequently on mine. He belonged to AA externally, but internally he had never really joined.

Any AA member would confirm that many men joined Alcoholics Anonymous in order to win back their wives and to gain respectability in the eyes of the courts. The latter aided them in beating the many bad checks they cashed.

But Ted was another story.

"Shirley is asleep, Ted, and I don't think she's at all well."

"I'm sorry to hear that. Is there anything I can do?"

"I don't know. If I do need you, I'll call you. I must go now, because I want to be ready when she awakens, and you know it's impossible to tell when she's really asleep. It will be bad for me if she catches me on the phone."

How true this had been. The acute sense of hearing Shirley

developed when taking some kinds of medication was unbelievable.

I remembered a time when I was talking to my son, Jim, in what I thought was a low voice. Two doors were closed between Shirley and us, yet she heard every word we spoke.

When a spell like this came on, I had to be on guard, because if there was anything that would begin an irrational tantrum, it would be the suspicion on Shirley's part that I had been talking about her.

After hanging up the phone, I hurriedly began putting away the rest of the breakable bric-a-brac, and then decided to call up George, a cousin of mine, who was in the Navy.

"George?"

"Oh, hi, Mary. I was thinking about you. Where have you been keeping yourself? How is everything?"

"Not good at all, George." I was near the breaking point with George, my guard down, and my courage ebbing. He was such a wonderful person, so strong and patient, and always understanding.

"George, do you think you could come over to the apartment? Shirley is home and is not at all well."

"Oh, no, Mary. When did it start?"

"Almost as soon as we returned here this afternoon."

He understood perfectly, and it wasn't necessary for me to give any details as to how sick I thought she was.

"Mary, it's impossible for me to come. I have the watch tonight at the shipyard. Now listen to me for a few moments. I know you can't talk too long. Can she hear us?"

"I don't know, of course, but she does appear to be sound asleep."

"All right. Do you think you could get her back to the hospital right away?"

"No. She would never go voluntarily when she's in a state like this."

"Couldn't you threaten her? Tell her she must go back there tonight or else they won't let her out again next weekend?"

"That's just the trouble. Believe it or not, they gave her an overnight permission without even telling me. Well, George, I'll manage somehow. Thank you."

"Mary," he said stridently, "you can't manage alone. Isn't there any man who will come out and help you? How about Arnold?"

"He had to go out of town. Ted called me, however. Do you think I should call him back and see if there might be a chance of his helping me?"

"If that's the best you can do, yes. But get someone. Promise me."

"All right. I'll call him."

"Remember, when you call me, just ask for the Duty Officer at the Shipyard and I'll return your call as soon as I can if I'm not there. Good luck, and I'll say a few prayers for you."

"Thank you, George. Goodbye."

George was the only person I knew who had the strength and decisiveness to cope with this problem, and he had to have the watch tonight. Well, I knew he was right. I needed to have a man with me. I was not physically strong enough to help her if she should fall.

"Ted, this is Mary. Could you come over soon?"

"Yes. I'll be there about six o'clock."

This was what he'd been waiting for—an excuse to come to the apartment. He probably thought I was exaggerating the problem, but when Shirley passed out this quickly I knew that a big blow might well be coming on.

I had to try to return her to the hospital. I didn't know how, but it must be done.

It was beginning again. I could hear her moving in the bedroom. Maybe she would be better for having slept a while.

I returned to the living room and casually sat down on the sofa pretending to read the paper again. I could hear Shirley shifting around the bedroom, probably making an effort to reach the door. She finally came out into the hall and placed her left hand on the wall opposite the bedroom to steady herself. Glancing in my direction, she saw I was reading the paper. I noticed she drew a deep breath as if pulling herself together before her grand entrance into the living room. As she walked toward me, I could see her movements were very stiff, and that she was apparently determined not to hit either wall. I didn't think she had yet reached the stage when she would pass through a door going back and forth like a pinball machine. Having made it to the living room, she immediately headed for the nearest chair.

"Hi, Mother. My, I was certainly tired. How long did I sleep?"

"Oh, about three quarters of an hour. Do you want to lie down for a while longer?"

That was a mistake. I could tell. Now anyone could tell she wasn't well. Her speech was very disturbed. But the pathetic thing about this very obvious fact was Shirley's belief that no one could detect such a deviation.

But I had made a mistake in suggesting she should lie down again. For if I persuaded her to rest now, she would undoubtedly wake up about eleven o'clock and go marching around for the remainder of the night. If I could keep her wide awake for a while, when night came, perhaps she would sleep right through. This then was my plan—to keep her moving about as long as I could, still hoping desperately, however, that in some way I could get her to return to the hospital.

But immediately, she said, "No. I don't want to lie down.

You wouldn't think I'd get this tired having been in the hospital, but the patients are yelling at all times of the day and night and I never rest there. Oh, goodness, I'd better start to set the table."

My heart sank. We were off again. "Why don't you just sit and read the paper, Shirley? I'll set the table. After all, you're the one who should be waited on this weekend."

I could tell my voice had too much tension revealing my anxiety and concern.

It was not surprising Shirley immediately observed this, and took my suggestion as a dare that she was not able to set the table. I knew she would insist now on having her own way, but I didn't believe I could bear the spectacle of watching her attempt to do the job.

She went to the china press and began to take out my best plates. They belonged to a set of Dresden, very precious to me since it had belonged to my mother. As Shirley unsteadily set the plates down on the table she turned to me. "No, mother. You go on reading the paper. I'll do this. You know you had promised me I could set the table."

And so I had, much to my chagrin.

I settled down with the paper, if you can settle down comfortably feeling as if you're sitting on a pincushion. Glancing over, under, and around the paper, I tried to watch her every movement. The best opportunity to observe her, of course, was when I turned a page.

There was a crash as I hid my face in my hands, and one of the dinner plates shattered on the floor. "Shirley," I screeched. "Oh, no."

By the time I reached the table, she was on her hands and knees attempting to pick up the pieces.

"Please, Shirley, let me set the table and you sit down for awhile."

Somehow she managed to stand up again. "No, mother. I'm going to set the table."

With her hands on my shoulders, she pushed me firmly back toward my chair and the paper. Finally, grabbing my elbow, she sat me down.

Things had reached the point of non-argumentation. If I protested too vigorously she would get exceedingly angry, and would step up her pace of setting the table, in which case there might very well be no china left. All I could do was clench my hands, hold my breath, and wait.

After a few minutes I could hear Shirley muttering under her breath. Her words were unintelligible. Then, abruptly, with the table half-set she turned and started towards the hall. Horrified, and almost frozen with fear and apprehension I said, "Shirley, where are you going?"

I thought, of course, she was headed towards taking more pills.

"Shut up, and mind your own business." This was flung loudly over her shoulder as she took big lurching strides out of the living room. She passed by the bathroom and turned left into the bedroom.

Almost at once, I heard a loud noise as if something was being thrown on the floor, and then the sound of bureau drawers being opened and slammed shut.

I placed my head in my hands, waiting for what was to come next. Suddenly, there was complete silence. I sidled over to the bedroom door and cautiously looked in.

She was stretched out on the bed again. One hand and arm were stretched rigidly up in the air, the other arm hanging off the side almost touching the floor with the hand twitching slightly. From her deep breathing, I could tell she was dead to the world. Shirley had found her pills.

Closing the bedroom door, I returned to the kitchen,

picked up the broom and began sweeping up the pieces of my Dresden plate. A few tears came to my eyes. I could never look at this china without thinking of my mother and all of her goodness.

I wondered what to do about the table. I could finish setting it, but when a disturbance such as this was taking place, the risk of destruction was so great it seemed foolhardy to continue. Besides, the way things were going, the possibility of sitting down to dinner seemed very remote. The only trouble was if I cleared the dining room table now, and she noticed it when she awoke, there might be a violent argument. I had decided to leave the table as it was when the doorbell rang.

I hadn't heard any car stop outside, nor anyone coming up the stairs, and the sound frightened me for a second. I went over and looked through the small window to see who was there.

CHAPTER 3

Iᴛ ᴡᴀꜱ Tᴇᴅ. "Well, you came at the right time."

"I came as fast as I could," he answered.

I took his coat and hung it up in the living room closet as he sat down.

"Would you care for something to drink?"

"Do you have any coffee? I could go for a cup of coffee."

"No, but I can make some in a few minutes."

He lit a cigarette and we talked of small things, while I made the coffee.

"Where is Shirley now?"

"She's in the bedroom, asleep."

"That's a good sign. Maybe she'll sleep it off."

"Wait a minute. She's in very bad shape, and it is mandatory that she be returned to the hospital. You'll have to take her back as soon as possible."

"All right. Let me take a look at her."

Ted went over to the bedroom door and slowly opened it, so that no noise was made. His eyes became accustomed to the darkened interior, and after watching her for several minutes he came back and sat down on the sofa. Just as he was settled, the bedroom door flew open and Shirley ran across the hall and into the bathroom and locked the door. I shuddered.

"What the hell was that?", said Ted.

"It was Shirley, of course. She just went into the bathroom and she's taking some more pills right now. I know."

"But she couldn't be there. She was sound asleep when I looked in the bedroom. It's unbelievable."

"Go back then, and look for yourself."

Ted went back and looked into the bedroom.

"Well, you're right, I guess. She's either in the bathroom, or else she fell out of the window."

"Do you know what I think she's been doing? I'll wager she was wide awake and listening to everything we said. Then when she heard you coming, she pretended to be asleep. You'll have a dreadful time getting her back to the hospital now. There's one thing for sure, Ted, you'll never trick her out of the apartment."

"But I saw her asleep. I was sure she was asleep, and almost before I got back to the sofa she was in the bathroom."

"You know how canny these people are. You have to get up pretty early in the morning to get ahead of Shirley."

Click. There went the doorknob. She was coming out of the bathroom. "Hi, Dad. When did you come?" She was playing the game all right. Pretending she hadn't even known he was here.

She walked up and kissed him on the cheek. He looked at her in amazement. Her appearance was really awful, and her gait unsteady. I could sense keenly the knowledge of the entire situation gradually flowing into his brain, much the same way that I observed someone beginning to blush. Shirley apparently sensed it, too.

"I know I look awful, Dad, but I just got up. I can really sleep here, you know, because it's so quiet and restful."

Written words could never convey the slurred articulation that was now in her voice. She sat down with us for a very few seconds. Whenever Shirley was in a state like this she could never remain still very long. And her limit was approaching.

When I knew the time for her next decisive movement was imminent, I could feel myself breathing faster and faster. Once Shirley had taken a definite new action, my heart, breath and nerves would return to their normal high tension level. I could almost see her eyes light upon something to do.

"Oh, I guess I'll finish setting the table for dinner. Are you going to stay for dinner, Dad?"

Then she began talking to herself in an undertone, not even waiting for Ted's answer.

I got up from my chair and began to walk over to the dining room. I was about to suggest perhaps I could help, thinking in that way I could save some of the china. Before I could open my mouth, she began to speak. "No, mother. You sit right down. I'll set the table and cook the dinner tonight."

Her voice had that "Don't cross me" sound. She would be difficult to handle from now on. Undoubtedly, she realized that all her faculties were not operating properly, and this was a defense mechanism to stop further questions or interference.

Now, when I said she could not be crossed, I meant just that. Her behavior would be unpredictable, and she would do physical harm to anyone who aroused her ire sufficiently. Many times I had awakened with black and blue marks from a similar episode on previous nights.

I went back and sat down on the sofa, utterly sick at heart. Ted and I said nothing. We remained frozen, and observed her actions. It was pathetic. Only a mother would understand. To have to watch a child of your own flesh and blood literally deteriorate before your eyes.

Strangely enough, no more china was destroyed and the table was finally set. Not straight, but set. This in itself was an achievement because every act she now performed was jerky and forceful. For instance, when Shirley opened the silver drawer, it was jerked out and slammed back with a bang.

She had turned her attention to the kitchen and was apparently attempting to get dinner. At intervals I could hear the refrigerator, door being pulled open and slammed shut. Pans fell on the floor, and now and then the water in the sink was turned on full force.

Ted and I were attempting to make some small talk as the table-setting neared its completion. When Shirley went into the kitchen, however, Ted asked me, "Have you looked for any of the pills?"

"Well, I've only searched the bathroom and found nothing. Of course, these pills are so small she can hide them anyplace. I haven't been able to look in the bedroom yet."

We had been talking in very low voices, so low I never thought she could hear us, particularly with all the noise she'd been making. Suddenly, Shirley wheeled out of the kitchen and yelled, "What are you saying about me now?"

"Why, nothing, Shirley." I tried to be matter-of-fact. "We were only concerned about your having to do all the work."

"Oh, no. Nothing doing. I told you I'd prepare dinner." She appeared to be satisfied and returned to the noisy business of preparing the meal.

Suddenly I remembered that in searching the bathroom before, I had neglected to check the clothes hamper. I walked over to Ted and whispered, "I'm going to check the hamper in the bathroom."

He got up and moved towards the kitchen to engage Shirley's attention, at the same time motioning to me to go into the bathroom and begin my search.

Ted certainly had to try to keep Shirley busy so I could do a thorough job.

I closed the door and began the tedious, careful search

through the hamper. I shook out every article of clothing, and painstakingly examined all those with pockets. Fifteen minutes were consumed and I had found nothing.

I had wanted to look in the bedroom, but when I came out in the hall I could see both Ted and Shirley were in the living room, and I realized she was now in a position to observe me if I continued on across the hall.

I joined them, at the same time pretending I hadn't heard anything they'd been talking about. I had caught a few words, however, and knew that Ted had broached the subject of Shirley's returning to the hospital. I heard her telling him how utterly ridiculous it was for her to return tonight. She stated furiously that she would go back tomorrow and not a minute before. Suddenly she became aware of my presence. Turning and looking at me with real hatred, she raged, "You! What have you been telling Dad when I was in the kitchen? That I've been taking pills, haven't you? Haven't you? Don't you lie to me. You just better watch out, you!"

If she'd had a gun, I'm sure she would have shot me on the spot. Her father attempted to quiet her down, and to restrain her from approaching me, but there was no way of putting an end to her raging and ranting.

Finally, he let her go. I stepped over in the corner of the room as she stomped by me into the bedroom, closing the door with a bang that shook the walls of the apartment.

"I'll tell you, Ted. This is going to be a long night."

"Don't you think she might go to bed now?"

"No, I think she's probably taking something else right now."

"Well, I'd better take the bull by the horns and go in and stop her."

"Go ahead, but she's so quick you wouldn't be able to catch her taking them. Personally, I'd be afraid to go into that bedroom right now."

"Maybe it would be better if she took something else—enough perhaps to send her back to sleep, or to calm her down so that I might be able to persuade her to get in the car and go for a ride. In that way I might get her back to the hospital."

It sounded slightly hopeful, but way inside, I knew things were developing into a pattern in which hope played little part.

Walking into the kitchen, I surveyed the wreckage that was everywhere. Tears began to come despite my efforts to remain calm. It was such a mess. The meat loaf had been cooked after a fashion and taken out of the oven. It was all over the broiler pan. She had evidently picked and eaten it with her fingers. A catsup bottle was overturned and the burner still glowed underneath a burned pan of carrots. The carrots had been frozen, and the empty package lay on the floor where it had been flung in the direction of the wastebasket. On the opposite counter from the stove was a half bottle of milk and a few empty glasses.

I began to try to clean up. The appearance of the meat loaf had destroyed any vestige of appetite I might have had and probably did away with the possibility of my feeling hungry again for the rest of the evening.

When I returned to the living room, I noticed Ted was in the hall, peering through the door of the bedroom. Seeing me, he closed the door quietly and came in and sat down.

"She is definitely and positively asleep this time," he said in a low voice.

"I hope you're right."

"I've been doing some thinking. I'll need help myself if events should make it possible for me to attempt returning her to the hospital. Perhaps I'll give this friend of mine a call."

"Do you think he'd be willing to help us?"

"I really believe he could help, but only in talking to her. I'm sure he'd try to convince her that it would be in her own best interest to return tonight. And he can be most persuasive with people like Shirley. He's had experience with problems of this nature."

"It would be wonderful if he could come over, anyway."

"I don't know if he would be willing to use physical force. However, even with two of us I'm not sure we'd be strong enough to manage Shirley. I'm afraid in the end we'd probably have to call the police."

Just what I had so desperately wanted to avoid, if at all feasible.

"All right. Call him, anyway, but remember the phone has an extension into the bedroom and she might listen in at any time."

Trying to telephone was always one of my greatest dangers. Shirley was keenly alert and aware of any sounds of voices. As I said before, she could actually hear from a closed door, even when I might be talking in little more than a whisper. Perhaps these sharpened senses were the only weapons left with which she could defend herself.

There were two reasons why my conversations with others frightened her. If Shirley could restrict the knowledge of each new failure to just me, then she could vehemently deny she'd taken an excessive dosage on any given day or at any specific time. Secondly, she never wanted to admit even to herself that incidents such as this one, had occurred. Therefore, her anger always flared with strong denials in regard to pills, and coupled with warnings against any insinuations that any excess medication had been taken. Her greatest fear, of course, was a quick early return to the hospital. This had to be avoided at all costs, for the consequences of a forced return were severe for any patient.

I watched Ted as he telephoned in the den, and silently prayed Shirley was still asleep and would remain so. If only she didn't hear his conversation. If this happened, all the furies of Hades would break loose. I couldn't hear what Ted was saying but knew he had reached his friend from the length of the conversation. It seemed a long time until he returned to the living room, although I'm sure it was only a few minutes.

"He was home, then, Ted?" I asked.

"Yes, and he said he'd be glad to come. He'll be here in about a half an hour."

"Do I know him?"

"No, I'm sure you don't. His name is Max Stoner. Maybe you've heard Shirley speak of him. He visited her regularly at the hospital during the past month."

"I believe I have heard her mention him. Well, perhaps with both of you here she can be persuaded to return tonight. I certainly hope so."

But deep down, I didn't expect any real help to come from Ted's friend. Still, I hoped against hope I might be wrong and that all this could be terminated and resolved at the hospital.

How could I hope, when all my senses of reasoning told me that Max probably had a backbone made of the same material as Ted's—gelatin. Well, perhaps I would be pleasantly surprised—and something good would happen.

I decided to make another pot of coffee, and Ted came out into the kitchen with me. We spoke very little, both of us listening keenly for any sound of Shirley's having awakened. We had just taken fresh cups of coffee into the living room when we heard a commotion in the bedroom. Then a loud crash. I immediately ran to the door, opened it, gasping, and even before I looked in cried, "Are you all right, Shirley?"

I saw she was leaning against the bureau, and had pulled a drawer out so far it had fallen on the floor. She slowly turned and faced me, and with sarcasm dripping from every word, she replied slowly and as distinctly as she was able, "Yes. And why don't you just close that door and mind your own business?"

"All right." My voice was shaking slightly. "I was only afraid you might have hurt yourself."

"Please close that door at once." She said this deliberately and firmly, each word picking up speed and increasing in decibels. "And get the hell out of this goddamned room."

I did just that, and quickly. The best possible thing now was not to antagonize her in any way whatsoever. Ted gave me one of those, "Better leave her alone" looks, and before he could say anything I said sharply, "Well, suppose she had fallen, and re-injured her knee or leg again? Remember the time she broke her wrist in two places? When she does this there's always the chance of another serious injury." I paused briefly. "We must get those pills; that's all there is to it. But how to find them and get to them!"

"Why? That's exactly the wrong thing to do. Let her take the pills. She'll pass out in a little while, and then Max and I can carry her into the car, and drive her back. I'd like her to be in this condition when she returns so they will realize at the hospital the seriousness of this addiction problem."

"Right now, I don't care what the hospital staff thinks. Don't you realize she doesn't know how much she's taken now? That she can cause real damage, that a terrible tragedy could occur?"

My voice had risen during the conversation and Ted answered with real irritation. "You asked me to come here, so listen to me. I'll take the responsibility. You know yourself that most times she simply falls asleep."

"Oh, yes. 72 hours later." I didn't mean to be sarcastic, and didn't say more. I couldn't antagonize him, since I really needed help. The dimensions of the problem were rapidly getting bigger and bigger. Physically I knew I could never handle Shirley alone. In this situation, I would have to accept help from any source, even from Ted.

Suddenly, the door to the bedroom opened slowly, and Shirley appeared, almost staggering. In a small, winsome, and inarticulate drawl she said, "Hi, Mother and Dad. Isn't it about time for dinner?"

Although neither of us had eaten anything, we said we had, and that we weren't hungry right now. She managed to get to a chair and sat, sprawled, staring at the floor.

Ted and I kept watching out of the corner of our eyes, waiting for her next move which we knew would come any minute. Abruptly, she got up and tried to take our cups and saucers into the kitchen. I wasn't too concerned about what would happen to them, because I had used old ones. One cup did drop as she entered the kitchen and we could hear her trying to pick up the pieces.

I was completely absorbed in my own thoughts now. At the moment I knew nothing could be accomplished by talking to her. I desperately wanted, however, to enter the bedroom and see what I could find, but if I went right now I would incur the antagonism of both of them, and Shirley might go into a raging tirade again. I had a strong intuitive feeling that it was necessary at all costs to find those pills as soon as possible.

After a few minutes of silence Ted went to the kitchen and I heard his voice rising shrilly to a high pitch. "Shirley. Put that bottle down and get a glass."

Ted reappeared and sat down on the sofa. In a disgusted tone, he said, "She was drinking milk right out of the bottle. She looked like an alcoholic draining a bottle of gin."

Just then we heard someone coming up the stairs. The doorbell rang and Ted got up to answer it.

CHAPTER 4

"HI, MAX. THIS is a pleasant surprise. It's good to see you."

I noticed Ted winked and jerked his head backwards during the greeting, trying to indicate Shirley was in the kitchen. Max returned the "hi" and acknowledged he'd received Ted's message by nodding his head slightly.

"Mary, I'd like you to meet a very good friend of mine, Max Stoner."

"I'm happy to meet you, Max." And he could make me happy if he were able to do something to help the present situation with Shirley.

"Oh, hi, Shirley," Max said casually, as she came teetering out of the kitchen.

"Oh, hello, Mr. Stoner." Her face had really dropped. She apparently didn't relish the idea of seeing him, because she quickly excused herself and maneuvered for the bedroom. She closed the door comparatively quietly and no sounds were heard from that direction.

I offered Max some coffee which he accepted, and when I returned with it, he and Ted were talking together in very low tones. The conversation ceased abruptly when they saw me, so I immediately withdrew on the pretext of getting cream and sugar, not wishing to interfere in any way with plans they might be making to take Shirley back to the hospital.

Max asked me to sit down with them when I returned, but I refused and said I'd like to do some straightening up in the kitchen.

It was a real mess again, and quite honestly I was ashamed for Max to see the condition in which she had left it. I couldn't help thinking how amazing it was that I could still be embarrassed with anyone under the existing circumstances.

Shirley had evidently picked up a whole roll of liverwurst and taken a huge bite without bothering to slice it. I threw the whole roll down the garbage disposal.

During the entire process of cleaning up, I could hear Ted and Max conversing in undertones. Perhaps they had really hit on some kind of a plan. I silently prayed it would be successful, whatever the idea might be.

They both said hello when I returned. Max smiled, but Ted's face was expressionless.

Ted spoke first.

"Max is going to talk to Shirley."

I answered quickly. "Fine, but please remember her personality has changed greatly, and she will be very devious in resisting any suggestion of going back to the hospital. In fact, she will be suspicious of any kind of so-called help at this point."

"Now, Mary," Max said in an unctuous and rather deprecating voice. "You just let me handle this problem. I think I know exactly what to do."

He sounded like the expert talking to a rank amateur; like a father talking to his three-year-old child. Inwardly amused, I said under my breath, "Okay, Mr. Know-it-all. May success be yours."

Aloud I tried to sound pleasant and appreciative.

"All right, Max. I know you've had experience talking to people like Shirley. I just thought I'd point out some factors you ought to know, and which might be helpful."

Max went and knocked on the bedroom door. I could hear a muffled voice answer from within. He opened the door, and all I heard of Max and Shirley's conversation was the greeting they exchanged, for he closed the door immediately.

With Max gone, Ted and I began to talk in earnest.

What is your real plan, Ted?"

"Well, Max is going to talk to Shirley."

"Yes, I know that, but then what?"

"Look, Mary. Let Max speak with her. Then he'll know how to operate."

"How to operate. Why, Ted, that isn't any plan. Haven't both of you together thought of anything positive? Have you impressed upon Max that her return to the hospital is the only solution?"

"Listen. Take my word for it. Let Max talk to Shirley. He'll persuade her."

"I wish it weren't so, Ted, but I'm skeptical."

"All right. Why don't you at least give him a chance?"

After that, I tried to converse in generalities, but underneath I was extremely worried. I felt no real solution existed. The depth of the problem was not apparent to Max, and all my intuitions told me he didn't have the necessary qualifications, at least not for this situation. I didn't mean to criticize or ridicule Max, but I could tell from his remarks he was like anyone else who was familiar with this problem, but who never has lived with it.

In order to understand all its nuances, the problem had to be lived with day by day, hour by hour, week by week without respite. It had to be lived and breathed over a long period before real understanding could be attained. This was experience I doubted Max had.

It seemed a paradox, but even my own memory dwarfed the horror of Shirley's sprees whenever things went smoothly for two weeks at home, or when she was in the hospital.

The bedroom was quiet except for the occasional sound of low voices. This was a bad sign and frightening to me. I knew the inner struggle Shirley was undergoing. She had to present a normal façade to Max. All her mental resources were aimed at controlling physical abnormalities in speech and thought. I knew she could maintain this pace for approximately fifteen or twenty minutes. Then a complete deterioration of all faculties occurred. Frequently she became violent and mean. Frightened, I was plain scared.

It was a wonder I could think at all, but a plan developed in my mind. I realized later how inept it was. At that time, however, it provided me with the means of concentrating on a goal.

If I could keep Max here for a short while longer, perhaps the first signs of the impending cyclone would erupt, and he would be able to see the true disaster path we were traveling. Actually, the disaster path I was traveling, for evidently no one else sensed the depths of the problem as I did.

My object, then, was to prolong Max's stay. I felt a little more secure having resolved upon an objective towards which I could plot a course.

Max was still in the bedroom talking with Shirley. This was good, and what I wanted, because I had to make him remain long enough for Shirley's reaction to set in. If he did stay, perhaps he would eventually sense within himself the impending doom which I felt had to become impregnated in him, in order for him to lead and influence Ted to act. Otherwise, Ted would be useless.

Ted was going to be of little assistance anyway. As usual, he'd put all his chips on someone else, and in this case they were on Max. If Max failed, Ted would let me down. This I knew.

What could I do? What could I do? I needed an idea in order to persuade Max to remain. Frantically, I racked my brain. I could offer him something to eat, or I could try to play cards with both Ted and Max. I stopped abruptly and said to myself, "Now, Mary, calm down. Don't get hysterical, because if you do, you lose. Take a deep breath and count to ten very slowly. Think! Think! Think!"

My mind seemed to be standing still. My brain was an empty void; it wouldn't function. Then suddenly, like the crack of a whip or a flash of lightning, something established itself at last in my mind.

I needed some cigarettes and a few other items in the grocery line. I could buy them at the nearby delicatessen. I hoped Max would be too polite to leave until I returned. Both he and Ted could stay and watch over Shirley until I got back. I couldn't very well stretch my visit to the store for more than twenty minutes to a half hour, as Ted knew it was a short distance away.

"Ted, I must go to the delicatessen. There are a few things I simply must get."

"Now wait, Mary, until Max comes out of the bedroom."

"No, I must go now. They'll be closing shortly, and there'll be no other way I can get the things then. It's the only store I've found close to here. I'll be back soon."

I stated the last slowly and emphatically, determined to overpower any objections he might have raised. Quickly I grabbed my coat and went to the door. I was calm and quiet so that no disturbance could be created. I didn't want Max to hear me leave. "I'll be back just as soon as possible."

I literally soft-shoed quickly down the stairs and ran to my car. I wanted to get away as soon as possible, before any possibility of my being recalled might occur.

After I turned the corner at the bottom of the street, I quickly pulled over to the curb and stopped. A reaction was setting in, which was to be expected, I imagine, due to the strains of the day. Despite my efforts, a few tears trickled down my cheeks. Not many—I didn't really break down and I knew I simply couldn't for my own sake.

Opening my purse to get a handkerchief, my eyes caught a sparkle of gold. Reaching in, my hand closed over a small locket I always carried with me. I opened it. Not that I could see anything. It was too dark, and my eyes had filled up again. But I knew what I was observing without actually seeing it—a small picture of my mother. I still missed her after all these years. My mind was transported to happier days, and it was only with a concerted effort that I put my memories in the back of my mind. In another couple of minutes, I was in control of myself, and I started out for the delicatessen.

Fortunately, there were quite a few people making purchases, so I wandered around at leisure and made a delayed selection. Finally, I bought a loaf of rye bread, the small sliced loaf that goes so well with cheese. Maybe Max would be tempted to have a sandwich. I remembered I needed steel wool. I doubted whether it could make a dent in cleaning the pan with the burned carrots, but I could try, anyway.

Gradually, I began to feel somewhat better. The normalcy of being around other people and concentrating on shopping began to raise my spirits. I also purchased liquid soap to wash the silk things, three cans of soup, crackers, cigarettes and some cheese to go with the rye bread. That should do it.

At the counter, I said to the man ringing up groceries, "Hi, Mr. Eastman. No, I haven't forgotten. You may deliver the paper every morning."

"Fine. We'll begin day after tomorrow. Will that be satisfactory?"

"Yes, indeed. I believe I'll take two chocolate bars with almonds, too."

Mr. Eastman packed up my purchases and I turned to leave. "Goodbye, Mr. Eastman. I'll be looking forward to having the paper."

I had acted very smoothly and could tell no strain or worry on my part showed during our conversation. I usually never showed distress, and when people knew my real situation they were always amazed at the normal, calm expression and poise I maintained. But underneath, little did they know, I was a mass of quivering jelly. I would never know why I didn't have ulcers, since they're supposedly caused by constant tension.

My true weakness was I knew, in utter honesty, I could never handle Shirley's problem alone. Yet because of my seeming outward calm, everyone thought I could manage somehow, and somehow I *had* managed.

So, back to the car I went, and then to God knew what. If it would only break down by the side of the road so that I would never have to return. I had a sudden desire to run and run and run.

~*~*~*~

The car, of course, did not break down, and in a few minutes I was parking in front of the apartment. I did feel a little rested from my twenty minutes away from the maelstrom.

Before I even got inside, Max was at the door to my apartment. "Oh, hello, Max. How is Shirley?" He must have been watching for me, because he opened the door as I reached the top of the stairs.

"Mary, she's not asleep, but I've been talking to her, as you know."

I put my package on the dining room table as he spoke. Intuitively, I dreaded to hear what was coming next.

"I just finished speaking to her and was waiting for you. I'm sorry, but I'll have to go home now. I'm already an hour late for an appointment."

My heart sank. I tried to think of what I might say in order to prevent his leaving now. "Oh, no, Max. Won't you give me your opinion before you go? Please wait for a few minutes. This girl is really sick, don't you think, and should be back in the hospital?"

"I've talked to her, and it's impossible for me to influence her to return. She just won't go. Furthermore, I don't believe she's that bad. Shirley has promised me she'll stay in bed, and not move around, and will take nothing in the line of medication, so you should have no difficulty the rest of the evening."

I was shocked at the general lack of comprehension on Max's part as to what was really going on. Perhaps he was just in a hurry to get to his appointment, and his whole speech was nothing but an act.

I replied with some indignation, "No difficulty! Have you seen her trying to walk around, Max? Surely you couldn't fail to realize how bad she is." I stopped there, abruptly, because I could tell it would be useless to continue talking to him. His mind was not only made up as to his going, but in addition I knew he would give no further help.

"Mary," he replied soothingly. "I think you're unduly worried and concerned about Shirley. She has promised me emphatically she will go to sleep immediately. Maybe if you had more confidence in her you wouldn't be alarmed this way. I'm sorry, but I'll definitely have to be on my way."

The last sentence was delivered with hard inflections in his voice and with the "stern father" type of expression. Seeing my face, he realized he'd been too severe and his whole manner changed. He became like a doctor consoling an unduly alarmed patient.

"Mary, if I can help you later tonight, please call me. But as I told you, please don't worry now. I'm sure everything will work out. Goodbye, Ted. I'll be in touch with you tomorrow."

"Good night, Max. Thank you for coming."

And Max was gone. The only good he did during his stay was to buy me a little time.

Ted and I sat down and said nothing for several minutes. Then he began telling me how sorry he was things had turned out as they had. Everything in general—it was terrible for me, he said. This was all old talk to me, for all of his previous actions belied the words of the moment. I didn't care nor could I listen to what he was saying. My only concern was with the problem at hand.

In order to understand the way Shirley had managed Max, she had to be lived with. I knew her so well, and realized she had obviously gotten through to Max, convincing him she would not get out of bed nor cause any further difficulty. She could sweet talk. She could smile. She could be naïve, and strangely enough, when you least expected it, she had the ability to suddenly control herself very well for a short span of time.

It took me about four years before I made a general rule to regard everything Shirley said as a possible falsehood. Anything I wanted to believe I had learned to check out. In theory, this was the solid rule under which I worked, but in practice I must admit sometimes I hadn't followed it.

I would be in situations every day with normal people where most of the things they stated were not lies or exaggerations. Thus, it was easy for me to believe some of the statements Shirley made were true. In fact, I used to firmly believe I was smart enough to discern falsehood from the truth with her. Unfortunately, I was wrong. I couldn't do it, nor, often, could the best of doctors. Shirley was far too clever to be outsmarted.

I was rudely roused from my thoughts. Like another roll of thunder, I heard the bathroom door close and the lock click again. Both Ted and I visibly started. He jumped to his feet and walked to the bathroom door.

"Shirley," he called quite loudly. "I thought you were going to stay in bed for the rest of the night? You promised Mr. Stoner, you know."

There was a silence before she replied. "I made no such promise. Can't I even go to the bathroom?"

Despite the slurred words, she used her hurt, indignant tone of voice. This was a sure sign to me that the second act was well on its way.

I was beginning to get frightened because instinctively I felt Ted was waiting for an opportune time to back out and depart. He was plainly showing signs of nervousness himself, and with Max's departure and his parting words, Ted might well take the same tack with me. I could sense it unmistakably.

Shirley was doing whatever she was doing in the bathroom with much running of water. This was always a giveaway that something was really happening. At last the bathroom door opened and she came into the living room. There was a wild look in her eyes, although she walked with some degree of controlled gait, probably due to her sojourn in bed.

"Boy," she slurred. "Mr. Stoner is certainly a very nice person. Have you known him long, Dad?"

"Yes, for quite some time now. He's very generous with his time and genuinely interested in people. I don't know anyone else who would leave guests to come and try to help you tonight."

"And how is your new little MG, Dad?"

She obviously wasn't listening, and I could tell her powers of concentration were almost gone. Her only approach now would be to ask questions and hope the answers would be very long so she wouldn't have to talk too much herself. By this time, she knew only too well her lips were no longer functioning with any degree of crispness. It would only be with a supreme effort on her part that a conversation could be made.

"Oh, the car is running fine."

I watched Ted during the conversation and could tell he was fully aware of what was transpiring. She was in the process of breaking up completely right in front of us. Her features and general appearance came close to approaching an animalistic level. It was heartbreaking, frightful and eerie.

Somehow she proceeded to the kitchen again—I supposed for something to eat, or because she could not remain still. As soon as she left the room, I said, "Ted, she has to go back to State Hospital. You simply can't sit here and watch her destroy herself in front of you. After all, you are her father."

"What am I to do?" he asked nervously and with irritation. "You know as well as I do it will take three or four people to even get her down to the car, much less into it, if she won't go of her own free will. And you know now she won't go voluntarily, Mary. If Max couldn't convince her to return, then no one will have any success. That I can guarantee you."

The last sentence was said rather loudly and Shirley poked her head around the door from the kitchen and asked, "Did someone get hurt?"

From here on it wouldn't matter what anyone said. Any conversation would presently be beyond her comprehension.

"Max," I said with some bitterness. "He was a flop—a complete flop."

I put my head in my hands. "My God, you're her father. Are you going to sit there and watch her destroy herself?"

"No!" And this was a shout. "Now, listen, Mary," he said more calmly. "I think the best idea of all is to let her go. Just let her go. Sooner or later, if she takes some more pills she will go to sleep. Then it will all be over until tomorrow morning, and we can make another plan of action."

"Well, I've seen and heard everything now. Suppose she falls on the floor? I'm not big enough to get her up and into bed. It's happened before as you well know." I was very angry.

"Then simply leave her there if she falls. She won't know the difference anyway. What does it matter if she's on a mattress or a bed of nails if it gets that bad?"

Almost simultaneously a loud crash came from the kitchen. Ted and I both rushed to the entrance and looked in. She was still on her feet, but the broiler had for some reason been pulled out from the oven, and had fallen on the floor. I had bought a cake in the morning, and cake crumbs were scattered everywhere. Some dirty towels were in the sink with two or three dishes and kitchen utensils to keep them company. She didn't even seem to be aware Ted and I were picking up the broiler.

Shaking, I stood up and told Shirley not to worry about it. She replied with what sounded like a mumbled thank-you and then proceeded back into the living room with Ted and me following. She sat down so heavily I wondered why she hadn't ended up on the floor directly underneath the seat. Ted and I both sank wearily on the sofa again. I glared at him with a shrug and an expression that begged, "Why don't you do something?"

My look was returned with one filled with irritation. He gritted his teeth, and I noticed he had begun to perspire slightly, which at least indicated some concern. Probably concern about how he could escape from the entire situation.

Shirley, meanwhile, was talking to Ted, and she was so bad now she thought she was talking with her brother, Jim. She asked questions about Gary, Indiana, and the duties of Jim's new job.

At first Ted raised his voice and replied shrilly that he was not Jim, then finally asked her whether she was crazy or not. It made no difference to Shirley. She just kept raving along by herself.

Ted then took a deep breath. I could see he was going to try a new tactic—reason. I'd heard this tried so many times before—the calm approach, the sweet approach, and I knew before it began it would be of no avail. "Shirley, dear. I really think it's time for you to go to bed. Especially if you want to get up early tomorrow, Sweetie."

No response.

"Now, your mother's very tired, Shirley, and I think we should all go to bed."

Still no response.

Signs of irritation were beginning to show again, as Ted got up and paced the floor.

"Shirley, as your father I insist you go directly to bed. This very minute."

Shirley did not respond again, nor did she show any signs of having heard a word Ted said.

"All right, Shirley. This is it. You will listen to me now. I want you to kiss your mother goodnight, and get ready for bed at once."

This was said with a combination of firmness and controlled patience. The latter, I could see, was about to explode any minute.

Still no response to the questions or orders, and all the time she was rambling away to herself. With each opening of her mouth now, a small amount of saliva bubbled at both corners. It was truly horrible to observe, and more horrible to be a part of the scene.

Ted finally stopped pacing and turned towards me. He was desperate now. He didn't know what to do nor where to look for help himself. He thought, strangely enough, that I possessed the answer to the problem. If it weren't so pathetic and desperate, it would be humorous. This incident had stripped him back to the child he always was. So very immature. And to think I had, in effect, married this baby.

In the back of my mind, I wondered in which direction his methods would turn; which way his head would eventually stop after spinning with a multitude of schemes and ideas. This was the way it had always been. Everything was a game of chance with Ted, rather like a wheel at the carnival which was spun round and round, and then came to rest on a particular number. So his thoughts would spin, then stop and go off in a different direction. The next day he would change, and the directly opposite tack would be approached.

"This is really horrible," Ted muttered to himself.

"You're so right," I agreed. "Where are you going to turn now?"

Then Shirley arose, stumbled towards the bathroom, and went in. This time she didn't lock the door. This meant she was in bad shape—in very bad shape.

I turned towards Ted and asked, "Couldn't you possibly get someone else over to help you?"

Ted didn't reply.

I persisted. "Perhaps there would be somebody who would help you get her into the car."

He still didn't answer. Desperately, I pleaded, "Please, Ted, can't you think of someone?"

Ted said nothing, but continued to stare, pretending to be lost in deep thought. Not that he wasn't trying to think at this point. Perhaps neither one of us was capable of thinking any more.

Changing the subject, I remarked, "I guess we might as well have some more coffee."

Anything, I thought, to try to keep moving and doing something normal. I heated the coffee and brought it out, and we sat for a time, saying nothing—drinking our coffee and smoking cigarettes.

When I returned from taking our cups out, Ted was trying to find his coat in the closet. I was completely shocked, and yet I shouldn't have been, for in a way it was an expected blow all along. I always knew he lacked courage and dependability. Nevertheless, there was always an inner glimmer of hope that this time he would show himself to be a real man.

"What are you going to do now?" My voice shook a little despite my efforts to control it.

"Oh, I have to get back to work or else I'll lose my job. You know that very well, Mary. I've told you before. I have the night shift at the motel this week, and I must be on duty at midnight."

I realized then that he'd never had any intention of going out of his way, either for me or for Shirley. He was so afraid of losing his job, so anxious to protect himself, that even the unfolding of this real tragedy with his daughter was of no paramount concern to him.

"You mean you are going to leave me alone here with this child?"

I couldn't believe it myself now, for Shirley was stumbling between the bathroom and the living room.

"I'm sorry, but I must get back to work. I'll call you as soon as possible after I reach the motel."

"A lot of good that will do. Thanks again, Ted. It always was your strong point—dependability." My sarcasm reflected my complete frustration.

"Here." I went to the closet door. "Take your coat and get out."

He quickly walked to the door, not saying a word, clearly relieved to have escaped any further responsibility.

CHAPTER 5

WE WERE ALONE again, Shirley and I, one person desperately wanting to help the other, and the other person deranged and totally unaware of reality. I sat down, and once again placed my head in my hands and tried to think calmly.

Down deep, I admitted I'd always known Ted would run out, but life and hope were strong factors in my make-up and I had, in desperation, permitted myself to think perhaps a change had taken place, and that in this time of real need and emergency, Ted would show some new strength.

I thought of praying, and repeated a prayer over and over again. It didn't seem to help me very much, and I knew I had to direct myself into another course of action and right away. I had to keep busy, very busy. If I didn't, I knew I would crack.

Clean the linen closet. That was it. Shirley must be lying down again for the apartment was very quiet at the moment. I worked frantically, as if my life depended on it.

The job completed, I decided to wax the kitchen floor. I had now gone into my all-night routine. There was nothing more I could do other than work as hard as I could. Previously, I had looked for pills and couldn't find any.

Shirley had enormous strength at times like these, so no one could force her to do anything she didn't want to do.

Thus, I could only hope against hope that she herself, and her actions, would resolve the situation.

I had purchased one of the new cleansers and waxers for floors, and decided to try it. It did work rather well, although I personally felt a good old-fashioned cleaning would have been better.

Every so often now, I could hear noises coming from the bedroom. Not very loud, but little disturbances such as an ashtray falling on the floor, or as if Shirley might have stumbled into a table. They made me shudder, but I was in a helpless position. All I could do was to be there—a living piece of furniture, an inanimate table.

Then suddenly complete quiet enveloped the apartment. It was striking because all the noises had stopped. I put away the waxer and ran into the bedroom. Shirley was lying on her bed, face down and breathing very heavily. I was both frightened and relieved. Frightened because of the heavy breathing, and relieved because she had finally collapsed.

Leaving the bedroom door open, I walked slowly into the living room. I was half-tempted to try calling the hospital to ask if there was some way I could get through to one of Shirley's doctors. I didn't follow through because I knew the possibility of contacting one would be remote and even if I were successful he would only say, "You'll have to call the police." I decided to wait a while and see what further developments took place.

I turned on the television and tried to watch a program, but every few minutes I walked to the bedroom door to check on Shirley. She was still sleeping heavily, and I hoped this would continue through the night.

I thought perhaps it might be safe for me to get ready for bed, so I undressed and went into the bathroom. While washing, I reminded myself to make one last attempt to find any pills. I made a real search this time, and after being unsuccessful again, went back to the living room to have a last cigarette before getting into bed. After I finished the cigarette, I remembered I hadn't brushed my teeth. I went back and used my electric toothbrush. The noise may have awakened Shirley, because as I was putting the brush back in its holder, I heard some movement, and Shirley came marching through the bedroom door.

I was finished. My shoulders sagged, and a complete feeling of hopelessness came over me. If such a slight noise as the electric toothbrush had aroused Shirley, then the night would be never-ending.

I tried to think. Maybe I should try calling the hospital after all. Before doing that, I decided to contact George at the Naval Base. He had given me a number different from his regular extension for tonight. Where had I put it? Now I remembered. It was in my purse. "May I speak to Commander Rig, please?"

"I'm sorry, but the Commander isn't here right now. May I take a message?"

"Yes, please. This is his cousin, Mary, and there is an emergency at my home right now. Will you ask him to call me as soon as he can, please?"

"Yes, indeed. The minute I can reach him. Good night."

"Thank you very much."

Wouldn't anything ever work out? Was it always to be this way? I, alone? No one to help. Just me versus a veritable tidal wave? This was a severe blow to my morale. I had counted on George. He always knew what to do. He always had a solution. It was not always the best solution, perhaps, but at least a workable one. George didn't talk, he acted. He had the ability to think and act simultaneously, so that something was always being accomplished, and this in itself made me feel better. I could sit and watch him, and see the problem being sifted in his mind and slowly solved in front of my eyes.

In retrospect, I should have known George could do nothing tonight. He was the officer on duty at the base, and this would have to take precedence over anything else. Had he known earlier, he might have been able to find a replacement, but the whole dreadful incident had occurred too late in the day to make this possible.

Shirley was now marching around the apartment. A different phase had begun. It probably was the result of having taken amphetamines. These pills made her hyperactive whereas the barbiturate family induced drowsiness and general apathy. In a rare moment, Shirley had told me that she took these different types of pills on an alternating schedule. If she realized she had taken too many barbiturates, she would then turn to the "pep" pill, to counteract her loss of equilibrium and sleepiness. In effect, she would try to balance the two, but in reality this was never achieved, for she couldn't control becoming either too somnolent or too hyperactive once she started taking medications.

I have said Shirley was marching around. She was, indeed, and now had a general determination like an insane soldier on the march into a bullet. If an end table was in her way, it fell. If she were looking for a sweater in a drawer and the drawer stuck in any way, it was jerked open violently and thrown on the floor or on the bed. Then, after a quick search, Shirley would leave half its contents on the floor or bed, the other half in a melee in the drawer. Bang—crash—and it was slammed back into the bureau again.

The drawers of her bureau were solid maple, and extremely heavy. Many a grown man couldn't handle them as she could. As a matter of fact, Shirley couldn't have either, had she not been under the influence of drugs. Then she handled them like matchboxes. It was no wonder she could completely overpower me physically.

She was now absolutely unmanageable. If I tried to restrain her she would brush me aside, as if I were a hanging branch blocking her path on a tramp through the woods. If I made any verbal objection, raised my voice in any way, she would probably have picked up the nearest object, whether it was a bowl or lamp, and hurled it at me. This had happened previously.

I had learned the hard way never to cross her or even appear to cross her in these circumstances. It was the latter factor I had to keep in mind. I always tried to stay out of the way due to previous experience, but on occasion might do something very innocently which was interpreted immediately antagonistically as opposition by Shirley. When her latent suspicions regarding my knowledge of the reason for her actions and behavior were aroused, I had to be on my guard.

I had my own analysis of the underlying causes for Shirley's basic antagonism and suspicious fears. Deep down she had an awareness of her misbehaviors, and was truly sorry for the trouble she had caused. But she didn't know how to get herself out of the mental abyss into which she had sunk. The result was she sank lower and lower. She thought she was climbing up and out, when in reality she was digging the pit deeper and deeper with every denial.

The solution, as I saw it, was very simple. Honesty. I believed I could have helped Shirley had she been able to be honest with me. She lied, however, with the same ease with which I breathed. Thus I became cagey in fighting to discern truth from falsehood. However, this was so alien to my basic make-up, Shirley could not fail to be cognizant of it. In truth, this factor of my personality and character only served to augment her duplicity and deceit.

Yet honesty would have resolved much of her problem. I can remember in Shirley's younger days, she once knocked over a vase while running through the house. It had been given to me by a very dear friend and was a treasured possession.

She came to me immediately in the kitchen, crying, and told me of the accident. Upset as I was, I put my arms around her, comforting her with the thought that we all make mistakes, that we all break things. How could I harbor any resentment against my child who was so obviously sincerely upset and completely honest?

Subconsciously, I had probably changed now, but so many things had affected me in recent years. There were at least fifteen cigarette burns in the new living room rug, and according to Shirley, I was responsible for all of them.

"You must have done that the other night," was her stock answer in accounting for any and all mishaps. Finally, I gave up asking any more questions.

The phone rang. My spirits lifted as I said to myself, "It must be George." I ran and picked up the receiver.

"Hello."

No answer.

"Hello. George?"

Still no answer, but I could distinctly hear someone breathing. What was wrong?

"Hello." I raised my voice.

At last a man answered. "Shirley?"

The intonation was slurred, almost inarticulate. Momentarily stupefied, all I could say again was, "Hello."

"I want to speak to Shirley. And right away."

I was shocked—dumbfounded, and frightened. "Who is this?" My words sounded harsh, almost hoarse.

"Never mind who it is. You just get Shirley on this phone and in a hurry."

There was something recognizable about his manner of speaking. At the moment, however, I couldn't put my finger on what it was.

Hesitating, not knowing what to say or do, I finally asked, "May I give her a message?"

Before the man could answer, Shirley suddenly burst into the den and yelled, "Is that my doctor you're talking to?"

Without giving me a chance to reply, she continued, angrily, "What are you saying about me now?"

The man on the phone broke in, shouting, "I heard her. I know she's there. Put her on right now if you know what's good for you and for her."

The tirade delivered, Shirley stomped out, slamming the den door behind her.

I was shaken and confused, feeling as if I were caught between two tornadoes. I asked as firmly as I could, "What is your name?"

"None of your G__ d___ business what my name is. But Shirley has something for me."

My blood froze. "What do you mean she has something for you?"

"She has my pills, and I'm coming over right now to pick them up. She was supposed to—"

I interrupted, "I'm calling the police. I don't care what she was supposed to do. Don't you dare come near here. If you do, they'll be waiting for you when you arrive."

There was a brief pause, then a click. He had hung up. Slowly, in a daze, I put the receiver back on the hook. I realized now why his voice had a familiar thickness, why his diction sounded strangely familiar. Whoever he was, he'd been taking medication, and plenty of it. His difficulty in speaking and slurred articulation sounded very much like Shirley.

CHAPTER 6

"So that was it all the time!" I said to myself. For the past seven or eight months at the other apartment where I used to live, there had been a series of phone calls which were, I thought, the work of a crank or potential thief.

The phone would ring. I would answer it and say, "Hello."

No one responded, even when I repeated the salutation two or three times. Yet someone was always there, because I could hear whoever it was breathing on the other end of the line. In a few minutes, the phone was hung up. After several calls like this, I would pick up the receiver and say nothing, hoping the other party would speak. Many times I was embarrassed when the calls were from friends of mine. They would naturally say, "Hello. Hello," and I would have to explain that I'd been momentarily distracted.

Jim had also experienced similar incidents with the "unknown caller." After talking it over together, we decided it was either a prankster or worse, a potential thief, trying to find out if any of us were at home.

There had been a series of robberies and many things had been missing from our apartment during this period. We thought someone had been breaking in when we were out.

We missed sweaters and other articles of clothing, but

precisely what was taken, we never positively ascertained because our life was very disorganized due to Shirley's illness.

Jim had called the police and asked if there was any way we could trace the calls. They explained the difficulties involved, and that nothing could be done.

But now I knew someone else was involved. In retrospect, I remembered Shirley had always tried to reach the telephone first. They must have had some pre-arranged signal. Tonight, however, he was apparently in bad shape, in such bad shape he didn't care.

What should I do? Call the police? Or was the stranger too frightened to come now?

I hurried into the living room and put the chain on the front door, deciding to take a chance he wouldn't bother us because of my threats.

I surveyed the overturned end table and scattered newspapers. The place was truly a shambles. The tension was becoming unbearable because I had lost all control over the situation.

I remembered George telling me when they were in the middle of battle during the War, they had a motto, "Do something—anything—even if it's wrong." I'd found this slogan eased bad situations in the past, but there was nothing I could do now—only stand and watch.

Shirley was in the kitchen again, eating, or rather I should say gobbling down food. It was an awful procedure to observe, and after remaining for a few minutes I couldn't stand the sight anymore.

Going back to the living room, I picked up the evening paper, and sat without reading, intent on the noises emanating from the kitchen. How long I remained there I don't know, but finally I was roused by Shirley rocking through the door into the dining room.

What a sight! Was this really my daughter, or was she someone else's? For the first time in my life I wondered if this were truly the child I had borne.

Shirley passed by without anything more than a mumble, and stumbled into the bathroom. Almost immediately she teetered out again, and into the bedroom. I surmised her medication must be there and probably should have followed her to try to see where it was hidden, but momentarily I was too exhausted.

She was moving around—I could hear that—and just as I was preparing to go in at last, she wobbled back to the bathroom, with her right hand shaped like a fist, and her right arm slightly extended.

Simultaneously the phone rang. I didn't answer it. I remained rooted where I was for fear it was the unknown caller again. He was certainly persistent—the phone kept ringing and ringing, over and over.

Suddenly I remembered. George would be returning my call. I ran towards the den but stopped halfway. I didn't want to hear that voice again. But the phone continued. Hesitantly, I walked in and lifted the receiver, but said nothing.

"Hello. Hello." A familiar and welcome voice.

"George! Thank God it's you. I've been so frightened."

"Mary, I'm sorry I couldn't take your call before but we had a fire on one of the ships and I couldn't possibly get away. Is it safe to talk?"

"Yes, George. She couldn't understand anything now. I'm so glad it's you. I had a terrifying telephone call a little while ago."

"Who called, Mary?"

"I don't know who it was. It was some acquaintance of Shirley's. He said he was coming over here for some pills Shirley had. He claimed they were his. I told him I was calling the police and he hung up."

"Good. Have they arrived yet?"

"You mean the police?"

"Yes."

"No. I didn't call. I did put the chain on the front door."

"Maybe you should call them, Mary."

"If he comes, I'll call them. He sounded pretty frightened when I mentioned sending for the law. I promise, George, I won't take the chain off for anyone."

"All right, but be careful. Are you taking Shirley back to the hospital?"

"I won't be able to, George. I'm all alone. Somehow I'll just have to try and survive the night."

"Didn't he come?"

"Oh, Ted came all right, but he had to go back to his job or he would be fired. At least that was his story." I said this rather bitterly. I would never understand her own father leaving her in this state.

"That dirty pig," ripped George. "What are you going to do now, Mary?"

"I wouldn't know, George. What would you advise?"

"Well, this would be my plan. I think you should at least get into your night clothes, brush your teeth and get ready for bed. Then if by any chance she should settle down and go to sleep, you can at least try to get some rest. Don't bother to try to clean anything up tonight. Leave it until tomorrow. Mary, it's paramount you get some rest if you have the opportunity. No one can possibly bear up under this strain."

This was spoken in a military manner, but with a genuine twist of gentleness.

"I am undressed, George, and I'll try to do as you say. Thanks for calling. I only wish you were here."

"So do I. Goodnight, Mary, and please take care of yourself."

"Goodnight, George."

Wearily, I hung up the receiver, slowly leaving the den. I went into the bedroom. There wasn't any hurry because Shirley would have to go to bed before I could settle in. Only when I could be sure she would remain in bed herself, was sleep a possibility for me. Maybe that would not be for another forty-eight hours. I really never knew, but was always so afraid of fire and other accidents, I never felt easy while she was up and about.

I went in my bathroom to get a drink of water and took a look at myself in the mirror. It was a tired face, a weary face, but not yet a completely defeated face. Rather, it looked like the sum total of a wooden deadness—a face upon which no emotion or event could leave its mark or pierce its set look of tired passivity.

What a contrast from this morning. Sleep, sleep, sleep. If she would only go to bed soon. I would be so happy. I decided to do as George had suggested, no more cleaning tonight. Underneath I was too weary and exhausted to attempt anything more.

Back in the bedroom I cleaned off my own bed, and put a few things back in the drawers. I didn't even bother with hers, and finally became so disgusted with the general disorder I threw some articles in one corner of the room.

I was very tired now, and wanted so much to rest. Perhaps I could stretch out on top of my bed for a few minutes. There wasn't anything I could do now anyway. I was neither strong enough to lift her and put her into bed, nor powerful enough to prevent her from any action which she might desire to pursue.

I lay down and propped two pillows under my head so under no circumstances would I drift off to sleep. I didn't get under the covers, just threw a comforter over my legs, and closed my eyes, listening for any unusual noise in the apartment.

Occasionally I thought I heard running water and the refrigerator door opening and closing. Sometimes I distinctly heard staggering footsteps from the kitchen to the bathroom, and back again.

Thud! What was that? I sprang off the bed and ran through the living room to the kitchen. There she was, lying on her back on the floor. Her shoulders projected slightly into the dining area, but the rest of her body was in the kitchen. Her left arm was at a forty-five-degree angle towards her feet, the right arm straight down by her side. Her head was twisted to one side.

I first looked for any noticeable injuries which might have been caused by the fall—abrasions or lacerations. Thank God, there were none I could see. During my examination, I called her name repeatedly, but she didn't answer. There was no response other than an unreasonably loud stentorian breathing. Very slow and regular, but extremely deep; in and out, as if some invisible force were administering artificial respiration by the chest method, but at a stronger and slower rate than normal.

Gently I raised her head and looked at the back of it, trying to observe whether she had hit it during her fall. There were no bumps or discolorations of any kind, and I must confess the possibility of a concussion didn't enter my mind. Finally, I felt reasonably sure no real damage had been done to her head.

It was a grotesque picture, to say the least. I desperately wanted to help her in some way. Taking her under both arms, I tried to shift, pull, and half-drag her into the living room, thinking I might be able to put her on the sofa, if I could gather the necessary strength. But she was all dead weight. The more I pulled and tried to move her, the deader the weight seemed to be. I only managed to move her a few feet from the position where she had fallen, so she remained in relatively the same spot.

Completely out of breath, I went over and slumped into a chair. Holding onto the arms tightly, I tried to get my mind to function again. It was temporarily a blank. Then I suddenly remembered Ted's telling me she would eventually pass out if I let her go. Well, she'd certainly passed out now.

For all practical purposes, she was dead. Her breathing was the predominant noise in the apartment—really the only noise, and consequently sounded all the louder to me. I tried to think the situation through as it now appeared to me, and finally reached a decision. I would let her "sleep it off" in her present position, since it was impossible for me to lift her. I grabbed a pillow and some blankets, thinking she might catch cold sleeping on the floor. Taking them back with me, I carefully lifted her head and laid it on the pillow. I tried to arrange one of the blankets underneath her body to protect her from any drafts. The other two I wrapped gently around her body.

After standing and watching her for several minutes, I went back and lay down on my bed for a while. I thought maybe I could sleep for a few minutes, but somehow, I couldn't throw off the feeling that this time there was something very wrong with Shirley.

I took two or three deep breaths, rolled over on my right side, and closed my eyes. My brain slowed down some, but never came to a real halt. It was a nagging mind, and down deep resided a real warning of disaster. Over and over my mind kept telling me to do something I wasn't doing. Perhaps it was only my imagination.

I couldn't relax because of the persistent conviction I shouldn't be in bed at this time. Finally, I gave up, dragged myself to my feet and went back into the kitchen to see Shirley. And what I saw frightened me.

At the most, I'd been gone only fifteen or twenty minutes, but what a change had taken place in so short a time. There was nothing new in Shirley's position. Her breathing was the same—perhaps a little heavier, but what frightened me so was the color of her face. It was definitely blue, and the discoloration wasn't due to a bruise or wound of any kind. Something was dreadfully wrong. I instinctively knew she was very sick. The poor girl. What was I to do? God, what a nightmare!

Was I right in my intuition about how ill she was? I felt helpless for a moment, not being able to think or act, but realizing that something needed to be done, and quickly. I thought of calling the police, but underneath I still was afraid of angering Shirley. I had been through so many vicious reprisals for calling in outside help before. This I wanted to avoid.

Sometimes in the past I had spoken to her doctors. When Shirley found out, she was furious. In justice, I used to be in a dilemma because I knew she was taking advantage of them, and getting too much medication. Thus, I would intercede in an attempt to prevent the doctors from being deceived. Evidently, their changed attitudes during her next visits made Shirley aware of my contact. Either that, or the doctors discussed my conversations with her. I don't know what she said to them, but no doctor ever listened to me a second time. As I said before, she could convert anyone to her own viewpoint.

I had vowed never to interfere nor become involved with her and her physicians again. The reactions and general upheaval weren't worth it. Besides, she was now under the care of doctors who were supposed to be familiar with this type of case, and it would seem they should be able to distinguish between the truths and untruths of her talks with them. I also felt any outburst provoked by my interference would only retard Shirley's progress.

Whether this was a true analysis of the reasons for my not calling the police at this time I would never know. Because any conclusion regarding my own actions would have to be tempered by the knowledge of what had been going on during the preceding hours in the apartment.

CHAPTER 7

HELPLESS, AND HOPELESS, I felt utterly lost, but I knew I had to act. I looked at Shirley again and almost panicked. Getting up, I walked over to her and thought of taking cold water and throwing it on her face. However, inside I knew this would never arouse her. She was too far gone. I never did fill the pan with water.

Wasn't there someone I could call for help? Suddenly I thought of Ann Stanford, a friend of mine who had always been very close to me. She had kindly stored many of my finest pieces of crystal and china in her home when I had first moved to an apartment. She also knew of Shirley's problem firsthand, and had helped me on a previous occasion. I hadn't talked with her for several days but this was normal in our relationship during recent months.

Ann was a registered nurse and of all the people I knew, she would be able to tell me how serious Shirley's present condition might be. I had forgotten her telephone number momentarily and had to look it up. When I finally found it, I wrote it down so I wouldn't forget while dialing. This wasn't a usual practice of mine, because I'd always had the ability to remember telephone numbers. Tonight I couldn't trust myself. I prayed she was at home, and if so, that she would come.

Ann's telephone rang several times, and I was afraid there would be no answer. I decided to let it ring at least ten more times before hanging up for I knew she and Ben had a telephone in their bedroom. If they were home, it would eventually awaken them.

On about the eighth ring, a muffled sleepy voice answered, "Hello."

"Ben. This is Mary."

"Yes, Mary."

I tried to be as calm as possible, and thought I was doing a good job of it despite the sense of urgency in my voice.

"What's the matter, Mary?" Ben was beginning to wake up.

"Ben, would it be at all possible for you and Ann to come over to my apartment right away? Shirley is lying on the floor and I think she might be dying. I don't know, but I would be ever so grateful if you would come, please."

I put every ounce of tensioned urgency into the word, "Please," I'm sure.

"Stay on that phone, Mary, until I return."

Instantly I knew Ben would come. I could hear him calling to Ann, and explaining the desperate situation at the apartment.

"Mary." He was back on the phone with me, thank God.

"Yes, Ben?"

"Will you tell me in detail the route to your new apartment, please? We don't know it too well, particularly at night."

I began to give him directions. He interrupted me a few times in order to clarify some of the turns he would have to make.

"Now, take it easy, Mary. We'll be there very soon."

He had hung up, but even before the conversation ended, I felt better. The knowledge that they would soon be on their way, and I would no longer be alone with Shirley made me momentarily happy, despite the circumstances of their coming.

Ben was a big, fine man, gentle and kind, and very firm. He would know what to do—the right thing to do. And Ann's calm judgment, both from a medical and a practical standpoint, would give me the additional strength I needed and relieve me of the heavy burden I had been carrying alone all night.

I began to put on all the lights, so Ben and Ann would be sure to know in which apartment I lived. There was a small balcony off the living room. I decided, cold as it was, to open the door a few inches so as to permit more light to be seen from the outside. Also, with the door open, I would be able to hear their car.

I kept busy, straightening any little thing I could find which seemed to be out of place. Every time I heard or imagined I heard a car drive up the hill, I ran out on the balcony. This was rather silly—they would hardly have had time to dress and leave home. I estimated it would take them a minimum of 15 minutes, and a maximum of 25 minutes to reach the apartment. At best, it would be a long waiting period for me, so I concentrated on remaining active in any way I could.

It was becoming extremely difficult for me to look at Shirley. She was so very motionless, and her breathing seemed more labored and heavy, almost as if it were coming from a strange place deep within her.

All of a sudden I realized music was blaring. The radio was on. When I had switched on the lights, the clock radio must have been connected in some way. I ran and quickly turned it off. All was quiet again, except for the frightening sound of Shirley's breathing.

I made a mental list of any medical equipment Ann might need and wondered if there were any preparations I might take care of before they arrived. I could think of nothing but blankets, and ran and got a couple more, putting one over Shirley's legs.

I hesitated to disturb her in her present condition. What had really happened, and how could I have resolved this whole dreadful emergency earlier? How? How?

I left Shirley, listening every minute for the sound of a car motor, and put away some kitchen silver.

Suddenly, they were here—I heard the car. Yes, there they were, parking right in front of the entrance to my apartment. I ran out on the balcony, so they'd surely know which side of the entrance to come in. I tried to smile as I waved to them. They had opened the foyer door now and were coming up the stairs. I met Ann at the front door and she threw her arms around me, hugging me tightly. Ben brushed a brotherly kiss across my cheek, patted my back and closed the door behind us. I was about ready to spill over with tears of gratitude. I was no longer alone. I was no longer alone.

Unable to speak, I pointed to where Shirley was lying. Ben and Ann both went over immediately and knelt down beside her. Ann took her pulse, and it seemed scarcely a minute before she turned to Ben and said in a low, firm voice, "Ben. Call an ambulance at once."

I knew now Shirley must be very sick indeed, and was only thankful Ben and Ann knew all of the details of her case, and were completely aware of all the circumstances involved.

"Mary, do you know the number of the State Hospital?" Ben asked me very calmly, but with real urgency. it was a relief to have an honest-to-goodness man taking charge at last. I couldn't have handled any more pressure at this moment.

I gave Ben the number of the hospital, and led the way

to the telephone. As he was placing the call, I went back to Ann and asked if I might be able to help her in any way. She suggested I get a pan of water and a face cloth, and also asked for another pillow to put under Shirley's feet. On my way to the linen closet, I heard Ben's voice—controlled but angry and firm.

"If you don't connect me with the doctor on duty, you won't be working there tomorrow. I'll see to that personally."

I had to stop and listen. There was a pause between answers on the telephone.

"Dr. Pusey? This is Mr. Stanford. There's a patient from your hospital here, a Shirley Daniels, and she's in a complete coma from an overdose of medication. We will be bringing her in shortly in an ambulance. You had best make the necessary preparations there, because as fast as the ambulance can arrive, she will be at the hospital."

Ben hung up the phone. I had the pillow now and was on my way back to Ann. Ben called to me, "Mary, where's the telephone book?" I quickly ran back and gave it to him.

Flipping open the cover, he found the number of the local police and began to dial.

"This is Mr. Ben Stanford at 28 Mendel Road, Apartment A. There's an emergency here; a young lady in serious condition. She's in a complete coma from an overdose of medication. We don't know what type, or what else she may have taken. Will you come immediately, please?"

Apparently the officer was asking Ben some questions because there was a pause in his conversation. "Yes, my name is Mr. Stanford. It's definitely serious and we will undoubtedly need oxygen. Will you call the ambulance service or shall I? You'll call it? Thank you very much, officer."

Ben turned to me. "Mary, is there anyone else that should be contacted at this time?"

I thought for a minute.

"Yes, would you call George Rig, please? He's on duty at the Naval Base tonight, but he'll want to know what's happening and the recent developments."

I gave Ben the number and the special extension in order to reach George. He was there.

"George, this is Ben Stanford. Ann and I are with Mary. Yes, Shirley is in a complete coma—very serious condition, I would say. She is definitely going to be taken back to the State Hospital. The police and ambulance will be here any minute now. I've already called them and the hospital. The State Hospital wanted me to take her to Memorial, but they're responsible, in my book. I finally hung up on them, and told them they'd better be ready for her when we arrived."

There was a brief pause.

"Oh, you're welcome, George. I, too, wish you were here. We'll keep in touch."

Ben came over to me and gently led me to the sofa. "Please sit down now, Mary. There's nothing more we can do at this moment."

He patted my hand and returned to Ann who was still kneeling by Shirley. Ann was desperately trying to get some type of reaction. She was calling Shirley's name, patting her hands, shaking her arm gently—but it was completely hopeless and useless. She frequently took her pulse, I noticed, and was watching her respiration closely. Shirley's color was decidedly worse. She seemed to be getting bluer and her entire face was puffed. It appeared to be almost swollen.

We didn't attempt to carry on a conversation. We all knew nothing could be done here and it was now a question of waiting for the ambulance to arrive.

In about five minutes—maybe more—I heard the siren. I

shuddered. A welcome sound, but all too familiar. How often I had heard it before!

The wail came closer and closer. Ben went out on the balcony just as the car reached the front of the apartment. I followed him. It was the police. Ben motioned to them, indicating the entrance they were to use; he let them in the front door a few seconds later.

The police realized at once they could accomplish nothing in a medical way, but began to ask questions of Ben and me and to take various notes. Fortunately, Ben handled most of the inquiries. They were both extremely gentle and kind. I remembered advice my father had given to us when we were growing up. "If you are ever in any kind of difficulty—real difficulty—always call the police. They'll be more than willing always to render help if you ask, and in far more situations than most people realize."

I knew now how true his counsel had been.

The sound of another siren was in the distance. It, too, was coming closer and closer. What a nightmare! One of the policemen went downstairs to meet the ambulance, advising them to bring oxygen upstairs at once.

The ambulance crew was wonderful. They were members of the neighborhood volunteer rescue squad. Ann introduced herself, and informed them she was a registered nurse. Oxygen was administered immediately to Shirley. It was everyone's hope, I'm sure, to revive her before moving her onto the stretcher.

After several minutes, it was apparent she couldn't be resuscitated, and Shirley was lifted onto the litter. I watched as I had watched before, but with a terrifying intuition that this time was as serious as any previous emergency, perhaps more so. It was a ritual—a bad dream dreamt many times before.

The furniture was pushed out of the way, the cloth put on the rug for the stretcher.

Shirley looked terrible, and my conscience nagged me as to whether I had done everything I could for her. I stood by the door as they took her out. The fast periodic flashing of red lights from both the police car and the ambulance gave an almost surrealistic look to the apartment.

Everyone felt it would be best if Ann rode with Shirley in the ambulance. I was to go with Ben. The apartment steps were quite steep and narrow, and with two landings to maneuver, it had not been an easy task carrying Shirley to the front door.

I followed the stretcher out of the apartment. Ann was ahead of me. When I saw the number of people crowded around the door watching this real tragedy, I wondered where they could have come from. The curiosity and morbid interest of adults was puzzling. Ben was behind me, and noticing it all, immediately understood. He gently grabbed my shoulders and pivoted me back upstairs and into the apartment.

I was deeply grateful, for I knew I would break down if I had to face such a big crowd. No matter how bad the situation, human feelings seemed to rise to the surface at grotesque moments. These crass curiosity-seekers shouldn't have but did embarrass and upset me.

Ben suggested I get my coat and purse. We heard the ambulance leave, but made no comment. In a minute, a knock on the door introduced the policemen again. They asked for my phone number and inquired as to whether there was anything else they might do to help. Ben assured them he'd see that I reached the hospital safely, and thanked them for their understanding and help.

After they left, Ben reminded me it was a very cold night. I ran back to the bedroom for a wool scarf. We were ready to leave when I noticed Ann had left her purse on the floor where Shirley had been lying. Despite precautions, the stretcher had left some grease marks on my new gold carpeting.

Somehow, Ben guided me out of the apartment, down the steps and into his car, and we began the drive to State Hospital. It was about one o'clock in the morning, and there were very few cars. Many of the traffic lights, I noticed, had been placed on the "caution" signal, and we were able to move at an excellent rate of speed. During the ride, I tried as best I could to outline the events which had occurred during the previous hours.

Occasionally, Ben would ask a question. "Did you find any of the pills Shirley was taking, Mary?"

"Not at any time, Ben."

"When did you pick her up today?"

"This morning, about half past nine. We had a lovely time together at luncheon, too, really a party at the Scandinavian."

It was good to be able to talk to Ben.

"I know how hard it must be for you to talk about it right now, Mary, but do you have any idea what she might have taken?"

"It could be many different kinds of pills, either a combination of several or a single drug. And I had a most ominous phone call in addition tonight." I proceeded to tell Ben all about the unknown caller and began to be visibly upset.

Ben changed the subject. "How's Jim doing?"

"He seems to be doing very well."

"Does he like his new job?"

"Very much, Ben. I only wish it weren't so far away."

He patted my hand. "You're a brave woman, Mary. Ann and I often talk about you."

Brave? If he only knew. No one ever felt less courageous underneath than I did at that moment.

It was wonderful to tell someone the whole story; wonderful expressing some of the inner emotions and feelings I'd experienced throughout the long, long day with a trusted friend.

Ben was very kind, but I could tell, despite his great composure and outward calm, he was most concerned.

Continuously, in the back of my mind, I worried about Shirley, a nagging, truly desperate worry. I was afraid to ask Ben the fateful question, whether he thought Shirley would live. I kept wondering what had set this whole dreadful chain of events in motion. Had I been responsible? Why hadn't I been able to find a single pill? Why hadn't I thought of calling Ann and Ben sooner? A thousand questions and fears plagued my mind.

~*~*~*~

In retrospect, I knew had they come earlier, even they could have done nothing until she was literally helpless. But if I had only thought of calling them first, before I had gone to bed for those few minutes. That extra fifteen minutes might have been the difference now between life and death for Shirley. Or perhaps I should have called the police myself. Oftentimes in the past, things had worked out all right, but this was most definitely a time when I should have called them.

My mind was filled with divergent thoughts. It seemed as if my head was weighted with lead. I opened the window on my side of the car, and put my face into the wind, hoping the cold winter air might help.

Finally, we arrived at the hospital. I saw the ambulance standing in front of the main entrance. Ben parked directly behind it. We both got out simultaneously, not saying a word, intent on what was awaiting us inside.

Entering the lobby, we noticed feverish activity outside the receiving room. The ambulance driver was standing in the midst of the activity of nurses, who were running in and out. Ben must have had a premonition. He walked up to the driver and asked him not to leave until we knew the final disposition of Shirley.

CHAPTER 8

WE ENTERED THE receiving room. Shirley was lying on the table, her mouth packed with cotton and tubes in her nostrils. The doctors on duty—there were two of them, very young, and not a little frightened—did not lend any confidence to the picture. They were pumping her stomach and attempting to obtain a reaction from her. In between they kept asking me various questions.

"What did she take?"

"Do you know whether she had access to barbiturates?"

"Has she ever taken amphetamines or tranquilizers?"

"Was there any way at all she had access to any of these pills?"

"Do you know if she'd been drinking? We are sure she has alcohol on her breath."

We were there about a half an hour. Work was going on with the stomach pump at a frantic pace. But somehow it didn't seem that long to me. I could see they had managed to get some results with the pump.

During this time Ben left and telephoned his daughter, Marilyn, who was home alone. He wanted to check to be sure she was all right, and to tell her they'd be home soon.

Between answering the doctors' questions to the best of

my ability, I kept asking myself the question, "Why did all this happen to Shirley and me?"

Why? What was the answer to it all? Everything gradually became a mental blur. But then abruptly the pace changed.

It was the doctor speaking—the older of the two.

"Miss Smith. Get me Memorial Hospital Emergency immediately on the telephone, please. Tell them we have a patient in complete coma—overdose of pills and probably alcohol, and tell them we are sending her over there at once. There's nothing more we can do here; we're not equipped to handle a case of this gravity. Keep the line open and I'll be in to talk to them shortly to give additional information."

The doctors and nurses at State Hospital had constantly attempted to obtain some type of reaction from Shirley. I was asked to call her name in an effort to arouse her. The doctors scratched her feet and also continuously called to her; they frequently lifted her eyelids and examined her pupils with a bright light. It was all to no avail. She never responded.

Finally, they moved her back into the ambulance and Ann accompanied her on her way to Memorial Hospital. Ben and I remained behind a few minutes, answering further questions asked by the doctors. Then we, too, left for Memorial.

During the drive, we were silent most of the way; I with my thoughts, Ben with his. I was so grateful to Ben and Ann for the help I desperately needed, and I knew I would never know how to express my thankfulness for their kindness.

Occasionally, Ben would say something encouraging to me, "Memorial is a fine hospital, Mary. If anyone can do anything at this point to help Shirley, the doctors there can."

I began to fully realize the gravity of the situation during the drive. A cold calmness gradually came over me. I knew

I would have to expect the very worst now. How it would all end I didn't know.

Due to the late hour, we parked in the space reserved for doctors, and walked into the Emergency Ward.

"Is there anything I can do to help you?" asked a nurse. I was frightened because it was so quiet. Where was Shirley? Certainly if she were here, it could not be this still; there would be some activity. And where was Ann?

I began to panic, when Ben said, "Yes, you can help us. We're inquiring about Shirley Daniels. Where is she?"

"Oh yes. She was taken immediately upstairs to the Intensive Care Unit. Are you Mr. Daniels?"

"No, I'm a friend of the family. But this is her mother, Mrs. Daniels."

Ben and I started towards the elevators down the hall. The Intensive Care Unit was on the fourth floor. How well I knew. I'd been there several times before with Shirley.

Before we'd gone very far, the nurse called to me, "Mrs. Daniels, will you come with me for a few minutes, please? We'll have to get some important information from you."

"Yes. All right." I turned around reluctantly, wondering what was transpiring on the fourth floor. Ben spoke to me as if reading my thoughts.

"Try not to worry now, Mary. I'll go on upstairs and see how things are going."

"Thank you, Ben. I'll be with you as soon as possible."

The nurse led me back to the desk at the entrance to the Emergency Ward. The usual routine admitting questions were asked. The nurse wanted her Blue Cross and Blue Shield number, which I didn't know. Then came a question for which I was totally unprepared, "And whom do you wish to have called as her admitting doctor? Some doctor has to admit her, you know."

I was completely at a loss. Shirley had been a patient in State Hospital for some time, and hadn't had occasion to see any doctors other than those treating her there. In desperation, I finally gave the name of my own doctor. It seemed only a matter of seconds before the nurse returned and asked me to speak with him on the phone.

He was very kind and sympathetic as always, but definitely firm in his explanation and refusal to take Shirley as his patient. He recommended I call Dr. Bard, who had been Shirley's doctor for many months in past years, and who had committed her to the State Hospital.

Before placing the call to Dr. Bard, I asked the nurse whether a priest shouldn't be called to administer the last rites to Shirley. I had dreaded to present the question, and was genuinely relieved when she told me a priest had been called at the request of Mrs. Stanford upon Shirley's arrival at the Admissions desk.

The nurse then proceeded to call Dr. Bard and talked at length with him. For me, it seemed an endless wait until she came back to where I was standing in the hall. Meanwhile, my mind was up on the fourth floor and not in the Emergency Ward at all. Suddenly, I heard her voice and felt her hand on my arm, shaking me gently as if to arouse me from my stupor. "Dr. Bard would like to speak with you, Mrs. Daniels. He's on the telephone now."

She led me to an inner office. I picked up the receiver. "Hello, Dr. Bard."

"Mrs. Daniels. I have received as complete a report on Shirley as is possible at this time. After consulting with the nurses and doctors in attendance, I strongly feel Shirley should be placed on what is called General Ward care."

"What does that mean, Dr. Bard? She wouldn't have a personal physician in attendance?"

"That's right, Mrs. Daniels, but I believe it's the very best thing for Shirley at this time. Rather than assign any special doctors, the resident physicians or attending nurses could call anyone on the staff who might be needed."

There was a pause, and he added, "And she is going to need all the help and attention Memorial Hospital can give in a case of this kind."

A real chill of dread, fear and apprehension came over me. Dr. Bard began to say something else when I interrupted, "From your conversation and reports, is there anything definite you could tell me as to her condition?"

"From the reports I've received, I don't know if it is possible for her to make the grade or not. The doctors are very dubious about her chances of being able to pull out of this. But be assured everything is being done for her that is humanly or medically possible. The most competent professional knowledge available and constant attention is being given to her right now."

I suddenly realized I hadn't even been up to see her yet. "All right, doctor. Thank you very much and goodnight."

I turned away from the phone. Underneath, I had known for some time how very sick she was. All the previous actions at State Hospital had more than confirmed my fears. I walked slowly back to the nurse. "Will you need me for any more information, Miss Hobbs?"

"No, that will be all we'll need right now, Mrs. Daniels."

She was trying to comfort me, I knew, as she rang the bell. I tried to listen while we watched the floor indicator and waited for the elevator to stop on the ground floor.

"I know this, Miss Hobbs, and thank you for your kindness."

Somehow I got in and pushed the button for the fourth floor. Ben and Ann were waiting for me as I stepped out of the elevator. I didn't have to say anything because Ben immediately spoke, "The priest has been here, and there are doctors and nurses with her."

I choked up. "Thank you, Ann and Ben, oh so very much, for being here."

I held onto Ann's hand very hard, and they led me in the direction of the waiting room. I tried to sit down but couldn't, and went back out to the desk on the floor to ask the nurse if I might go in and see Shirley.

"There are so many people in there right now, Mrs. Daniels, and there's really nothing you can do. I honestly feel you would only be in the way if you tried to see her at this particular time. She's getting every kind of emergency care possible."

I turned away.

The nurse continued, "As soon as we think it best for you and for her, you will be informed and may go in. She is, as you know, completely unconscious, and wouldn't know you were there."

I thanked her, and went back to the waiting room and sat down opposite Ann and Ben.

None of us spoke for several minutes. We were all waiting— waiting for some word, and realizing all the time that a team of nurses and doctors were fighting to save Shirley's life. Finally, Ben said very quietly, "We are so very sorry, Mary, but Ann and I must go soon, as Marilyn is home alone tonight. We only wish we could stay with you as long as you might need us."

I was panic-stricken, knowing they would be leaving. I would be alone again. "I'm sorry, Ben. I didn't realize Marilyn was alone. I should have asked before. Thank you so much for coming and for staying with me this long."

They got up and put on their coats. As they were about to leave, a woman dressed in a white hospital coat appeared. I remembered her from a previous hospitalization. It was Dr. Turner, a very fine doctor. "Mrs. Daniels?"

I stood up. "I am Mrs. Daniels."

"Mrs. Daniels, your daughter is very critical. Could you tell us what kind or kinds of medication she has been taking?"

"No, I'm afraid I don't know, doctor."

"Did you find anything at all you could show me?"

"I looked everywhere I could think of several times, doctor, but never found a single pill."

"It is paramount we find out exactly what she has been taking if at all possible, so we can administer the proper antidote. Would it be feasible for you to go home and make another thorough search? Any information you could give us as to specifics would be of great help."

"I'll do my best, Dr. Turner. I'll go over the whole apartment again."

I could see Ben and Ann conversing together in low tones. Ben came over.

"Ann and I would like to go back out to the apartment with you, Mary. We'll phone Marilyn, see how she is, and tell her where we are should she need us. Perhaps with three of us looking we might uncover something. Nothing means more to all of us at this moment than Shirley."

"That would be wonderful, Ben."

Somehow, I got into my coat. We went down to the parking lot. All three of us climbed in the front seat and left the hospital.

CHAPTER 9

I WONDERED IF THE stomach specimen had specifically indicated the kind of medication Shirley had taken. "Ann, did they mention finding any particular drug or drugs when they pumped Shirley's stomach?"

"Yes. They mentioned barbiturates. But apparently they feel this is a combination of pills, and possibly alcohol, too."

Usually we would have driven slowly returning from an emergency visit to the hospital, but this wasn't true that night. We had a sense of urgency now because of the imminent search to be undertaken and the possible consequences of its success or failure upon Shirley's life.

Ann kept her arm around my shoulders all the way to the apartment. We talked very little after she had answered my question. But we did discuss the doctors' concern about the multiplicative effect alcohol had when taken with drugs. The mixture could cost Shirley her life. This didn't trouble me, at the time, because to my knowledge she couldn't have purchased any liquor during the day, nor had she had anything at the apartment so far as I knew.

Ben put the heater on. It had turned out to be a very cold and raw night, and I still had my window open. I hadn't realized how bitter it was until the warm air gauge was turned up, but I hadn't really been conscious of anything except the critical pressures of Shirley's condition.

At last we turned into the entrance drive of the Arms Apartments. It was very quiet. No one stared at us; no ambulance sirens screamed; no police cars blinked their lights. It was almost too quiet, by contrast with the other events of a few hours ago.

As we drove up the hill I could see all my lights were on. it looked as if I was having a very gay party. How far from the truth this was.

We stepped out of the car, walked in the entrance, and up the steps. There was no need to use my key. I had forgotten to lock the door when we left.

The apartment seemed strangely still and empty, after all the confusion, nightmare and chaos which had reigned within its walls for so many hours.

Despite all my efforts to clean during the preceding hours, everything seemed to be in a complete shambles. We took off our coats. I felt more in command of the situation for I knew Ann and Ben had no experience in a search of this kind. Inasmuch as pills were so minute, and could be secreted in unbelievably small places, I explained they would have to be very careful in their investigation, and advised them to overlook nothing. I gave some specific examples.

"You mean sometimes in the cuffs of jackets as well as in the linings of pockets?" Ben asked.

"Not only there, Ben, but also in every type of box, container, purse and even inside hat bands, let alone hat trimmings."

Then I remembered one of her favorite devices for hiding medication.

"If either of you see a piece of Kleenex that appears to have been used, or even a small piece of toilet paper, be sure to unwrap it. This is one of her favorite ways to conceal pills. Also, be sure to look underneath all the edges of the carpeting, in the back of the record player and in and under vases or pictures."

I asked Ann if she would start in the bathroom with the medicine cabinet, particularly to ascertain if Shirley might have transferred her pills to bottles containing regular patent medicines. I knew Ann was familiar with the colors of various drugs, and could make identifications quickly. If she found anything out of the ordinary, she was to show it to me, as I was now an expert in identifying medications.

Ben took the den for there were still many unpacked boxes there. With no money to furnish and decorate the room, I had left many of my things as they were when I moved in. It was best for Ben to take this assignment as it entailed much lifting.

I, myself, tackled the bedroom, because I sincerely felt if there were any pills around, the greatest chance of finding them would be there, and I was more experienced. There were all kinds of cases in the dresser drawers plus multitudinous boxes. I made up my mind to search every finger of every glove—to open each handkerchief and scarf—not to miss a nook or cranny or single article which might hold the information we wished to find.

Ann, Ben, and I began our task. And what a task it was. We couldn't proceed too quickly, because with haste it was too easy to overlook something which might be the clue and key to Shirley's recovery. Even so, we all three realized it was necessary to work with some dispatch, for every minute that went by was a crucial one at the hospital.

In the nervous concentration bound to accompany an assignment of this kind, we did many things which were foolish. We found ourselves shouting to each other, "Have you found anything yet?"

And knowing underneath if any one of us had found even a trace of a clue, he would have informed the others at once. Then we would quiet down, not saying anything for a short while. Unfortunately, I couldn't restrain myself on several occasions, and would go in and ask if either Ben or Ann had met with any success. In addition, in my anxiety lest they overlook a possible hiding place, I would suggest different places. Most of the time, they had already looked where I mentioned.

We had been searching for more than half an hour when Ann came in and announced she had completely scoured the bathroom. I asked if she would help me by going through the last two drawers of the chest. She began at once, and I turned my attention to the closet, and the scrutinizing of each shoe and the pockets of every dress. I was unsuccessful, but halfway through the dresses I had an idea.

"Ann, did you do the linen closet next to the bathroom?"

"No, I didn't, Mary. Foolish of me. I'll get at it the very second I finish this last drawer."

By the time I completed my job in the closet with all its places and means of concealment, Ann had checked through the linens. For some time, Ben could be heard moving things in and out of the cartons in the den. He apparently had had no success. The only audible sounds were those when he was lifting a heavy article or box.

At last the three of us were in the bedroom together, tired, discouraged, and with little or nothing to say. Each of us in turn admitted failure. We sat on the edge of the beds, trying to think of other possibilities while we were resting. After a few minutes, I suddenly remembered Shirley had frequently had one of her arms flopping over the side of the bed whenever she was lying down. Quickly I suggested to Ben that if he would move the bed we might find what we were looking for in the suitcases underneath.

As he pushed the bed out, I realized we had not checked the most obvious place of all. Without saying a word to either Ann or Ben, I lifted as best I could the mattress from the box spring, and immediately spotted a bottle, a whiskey bottle, pint size.

Where had she gotten it? Where? I stood holding the upper part of the mattress in the air, frozen with horror and disbelief. It was a terrible blow. Suddenly I began to shake. I was filled with apprehension, really terror-stricken, as my mind revolved and literally tasted each side of the multiplicative effect of alcohol and drugs taken together.

Ben immediately grabbed the bottle, putting it on top of the bureau. He continued the search under the mattress at a rapid pace. Time was passing quickly now. We had been gone from the hospital for a good hour.

"Let's give 15 more minutes to the living room and kitchen. If nothing else turns up, we'll call it quits." Ben was decisive and we all went into action again.

If we found anything more, good. If not, I knew I couldn't remain longer than fifteen more minutes looking for pills, when Shirley was at the hospital with God knows what happening.

The allotted time period passed. We had discovered nothing, and were very discouraged. It was no use. She had probably consumed all the medication she possessed.

"Mary, I'm sorry, but Ann and I will have to go on home now." Ben said this very consolingly. "We'll follow you until we come to our turn-off."

"Thanks, Ben."

I turned off all the lights this time except for one small

lamp in the living room. We went down the steps to the street. I kissed both of them goodnight. I know a few tears rolled down my cheeks onto Ann's, and I guess a few of hers may have rolled onto mine, too.

Somehow I started my car and went slowly down the hill towards the main highway. I expected the worst concerning Shirley's condition. The knowledge that her fate was now entirely in the hands of the medical staff at Memorial and that I could no longer exert any influence or control over the final outcome, had become all too realistic to me. Momentarily, I sank into a world of my own.

I came out of it as Ben blew his horn. They were going to turn off to go home now. I returned the surprisingly pleasant greeting—the sound was a warm one at this hour. A wave of loneliness came over me again, and almost mechanically I drove the many blocks to the hospital, proceeding directly in the elevator to the fourth floor.

My keyed-up excitement had left me. I was devoid of all emotion, despite the fact that I could comprehend events going on around me and anything that was said to me. Perhaps the lack of feeling was a saving factor right now.

As I stepped off the elevator Dr. Turner met me. She had apparently come from the Intensive Care Unit, and I sensed at once things were most critical. "Mrs. Daniels," she began, "I'm sorry."

I interrupted. "Hello, doctor. We were unable to find anything except one pint of whiskey—rather an empty bottle under a mattress. No pills at all. apparently, though, Shirley had drank all the liquor."

"Well, that will help some. It does confirm one definite suspicion we had. Would you mind coming with me to the sun porch, please?"

As we went, she held my elbow, guiding me along almost

as if I were an invalid and were trying to walk for the first time after a long stay in bed. I was grateful Dr. Turner was a woman. I didn't know whether she had any children, but she was certain to have some idea what I, as a mother, was experiencing at that moment.

We sat down side by side on the settee. She said nothing for a few moments. Then she turned to me, "Mrs. Daniels. I can't hold out too much hope for you. Shirley is in a very serious condition, and generally in cases of this gravity, patients have a very difficult time making it."

"Thank you for telling me, doctor. I'd assumed this was the case."

"We shall continue doing everything we can. I'll have to return now."

"Certainly, doctor. Thank you very much for all your efforts."

Somehow I couldn't cry or show any real feeling. I just kept looking straight ahead. After a time, I got up and began to walk the hospital corridors. Up and down; up and down; up and down.

I thought about today—about the wonderful time Shirley and I had had together at lunch. How we had laughed. Looking back, it had been the nicest morning I'd had with her in five years. A truly pleasant two hours! It all seemed years ago now—like a dream of a previous decade.

I looked at the clock in the corridor. Ten minutes past three in the morning. Going over to the nurses' station, I talked with Miss Brevoort, who was on duty. She had been most sympathetic. Even so, I dreaded having to ask her the questions I felt were necessary.

"Miss Brevoort, do you feel Shirley is so ill I should call her father?"

"Yes, Mrs. Daniels, I believe you should at once."

The answer came quickly and directly. I knew Shirley must be very low at this very moment. "Do you have change for a quarter, Miss Brevoort?"

I was fumbling in my wallet for a dime.

"Let me see, Mrs. Daniels." She opened her purse and began to go through her change pocket. She didn't have change for a quarter—only two dimes, but insisted I take both of them. She wouldn't hear of taking any money from me.

I walked slowly to the telephone booth.

"Ted, this is Mary." He had answered himself.

"Yes, Mary. How is Shirley?"

"I'm down at Memorial Hospital. I'm afraid Shirley is going to die. The nurse advised me to call you at once."

There was a silence from the other end of the line. A long silence.

"Did you hear me, Ted? The doctors and nurses don't think Shirley has a chance. You had best come at once."

He cleared his throat. "I don't know. I can't lose my job, and there's no one here to relieve me."

As well as I thought I knew him, this was almost unbelievable. "Listen, Ted. Did you really hear what I am telling you? Your daughter is dying. She may not live another 15 minutes."

"All right. All right. I'll see what I can do. I'll try to be there in about an hour."

I hung up. There wasn't any sense talking to him further, I knew. He was afraid of losing a fifty dollar a week job instead of being with his daughter when she was dying.

I took the other dime off the shelf by the telephone and dialed long distance. I placed a person-to-person call to Jim in Gary, and asked the operator to charge it to my home phone. Jim lived in a quasi-hotel for single men in Indiana. He didn't have a phone of his own. In order to reach him it would be necessary to get the switchboard at the hotel, an almost impossible feat at this hour. The operator rang and rang. It was closed as I had feared. I explained the nature of the emergency to the operator. She was most understanding, took the number of the hospital, and said she would reach Jim somehow, even with the assistance of the police.

George's face suddenly popped into my mind. I wanted to talk to him. I must reach him.

"Miss Brevoort, I'm sorry to bother you again. Would it be asking too much to call my cousin, George Rig, at the Naval Base, on the hospital phone?"

"Certainly you may. What's the number?"

I gave it to her and told her to ask for the Duty Officer. In a few minutes I was telling George everything. After we said goodbye, I somehow felt relieved, but wished with all my heart he was with me.

I tried to sit at the little table outside the nurses' station. It was no use. I had to keep walking—up and down, up and down the corridor. Dozens of thoughts crowded into my mind. I thought of my mother and father and what they would say if they were alive. The need for them had never seemed more acute. If only George were here.

I wondered if another try at life would have produced a better one. What was the reason for tragedies of this kind?

I remembered very keenly when Jim and Shirley were young and still in their cribs. Particularly, Shirley—how I would enter her room in the early morning and see her pudgy little hands on the railing of her crib. The minute I came into the room, she would begin to jump up and down and gurgle with laughter. Such a happy little girl—so lovable and affectionate.

Even with these thoughts it remained impossible for me to

cry. I recalled Shirley's graduation from Country Day School. How beautiful she had looked at the Senior Prom—how gay all her friends and she had been at the breakfast I'd given after the dance.

I was still pacing the corridor when I heard the phone ring at the nurses' station. Miss Brevoort answered and motioned me to come over.

"It's long distance for you, Mrs. Daniels."

I took the receiver outside the partitioned alcove.

"Mrs. Daniels?"

"Yes. This is Mrs. Daniels."

I heard a familiar voice.

"Mother." It was Jim.

"Oh, Jim."

"What's happened?"

"Oh, Jim. It's dreadful. I'm at Memorial Hospital. Shirley is in the Intensive Care Unit and isn't expected to live."

"What happened to her?"

"I went to pick her up this morning at State Hospital for the weekend. After we arrived home, she began to get sick with medication; we don't know what kind of pills. She also had liquor. She took an overdose of barbiturates and probably other pills. It's been horrible."

"Is anyone with you, mother?"

As best I could I explained the events of the evening, about Ann and Ben coming to the apartment, and of their having to return home.

"The worst part is, Jim, liquor and pills of the sort she has evidently taken have a multiplicative effect rather than an additive effect. She is absolutely comatose and they hold little or no hope, I'm sure."

"I'll call the airport at once and get the first plane out. Is George with you?"

"No. He has the duty at the Base tonight. He couldn't come. I've talked to him, though."

"You're all alone, then. I think you'd better call Dad. It's only fair he be there."

I waited a moment before I answered, wondering how to tell him. "He was over at the apartment earlier in the evening when Shirley was very bad. Then he had to go to work and—"

Exploding, Jim interjected, "You mean he walked out on you and left you to handle it!"

Hesitatingly, I answered, "Yes, and I did call him when we first arrived at Memorial. He said he would come over if he could find a substitute."

"That son-of-a-bitch. O.K., mother. I'll be on my way."

"Wait a second, Jim. I don't think you should come right now. Don't misunderstand me, but this crisis will swing either one way or the other within the next few hours. If Shirley makes it, it will be fine, and there would be no need in your coming at this time. If she doesn't—"

I was fighting back my tears.

"Do you want to tell me any more about everything that happened, Mother?"

This was spoken in a kindly endearing manner, as only Jim could speak at times.

I did tell him more of the details, mentioning again how wonderful Ann and Ben had been to me. I didn't comment on Ted's friend, Max. There didn't seem to be any need for this.

"If things take a bad turn, don't hesitate to call me at once."

"I will, Jim."

"Please take care of yourself, mother."

"Yes, Jim."

"Now don't forget. I'll want to know, and don't hesitate to contact the Gary police again."

"I won't. Thank you. Goodbye, Jim."

The receiver clicked. Jim had hung up.

"Jim, Jim, Jim. How lonely and hard it is without you. How I wish you were here. I never needed you more than now."

CHAPTER 10

I HAD STARTED PACING again. It was a solitary vigil.

"Mrs. Daniels." Miss Brevoort had returned to her station.

"Yes."

"Would you care to go back and see your daughter now? The doctors feel it would be advisable if you feel up to it."

"Yes, I would like to very much, if I won't be in anyone's way."

"It will be all right, Mrs. Daniels. Will you come with me, please?"

We walked down the hall to the Intensive Care Unit. In the middle of the corridor were two desks. Equipment and machines were standing outside various rooms—oxygen tanks—all kinds of mysterious looking instruments.

As we approached Shirley's room, two doctors and two nurses came out. Miss Brevoort took my hand and led me in.

There she was, completely filled with various tubes and packings. She was totally unconscious. Miss Brevoort patted my shoulder and left me alone.

I walked over and touched Shirley's face very gently, seeing again, regardless of the bloated look, the packings and tubes, a beautiful young girl graduating from Country Day School in her lovely white dress. So happy, so excited, not looking

back but rather forward to next Fall when she would enter a
new phase of life—college.

I began to think about my own childhood. Scenes floated
in front of me. It had been such a perfect one in every way. I
remembered during the Spring thaw, when I would walk home
from school, how I would throw a stick, a very small stick, into
the running waters flowing by the curb of the street. It seemed
only yesterday I saw the snow on top of the curbing, and then
a clear span where there was water, sometimes bridged by
a thin coating of ice; and then more snow about six inches
away. The stream of water would, of course, continue on its
way to some destination—I didn't really know where. I would
imagine the stick was a type of big boat, shooting the rapids,
then going through big lakes. Occasionally, my imaginary
boat caught on some promontory, and I would reach over
and send it on its way again. Nothing could make me take my
eyes off of it as I ran alongside the curbing. I was so absorbed
in the journey of the little stick, nothing else attracted my
attention.

Once when I arrived home, my father told me he had
watched my little game for ten minutes. I remember him
asking, "What were you doing along the curbing this afternoon
for so long, Mary?"

I was embarrassed, and answered, "Oh, nothing
important—really, Daddy."

He then told me he had called to me several times. I'd been
so absorbed in the world I had made, I hadn't heard him. How
like life my imaginary boat trips had been! Never knowing
what lay ahead; being caught in situations where apparently
nothing could be done; never perceiving the outcome of
events.

Obviously, things were not going well or they wouldn't
have suggested my seeing Shirley. Possibly ten minutes had

passed when I noticed a nurse standing in the doorway. She gave me a nod, and I knew they wished me to leave.

I leaned over and gave Shirley a kiss on her forehead. She was absolutely inert; completely unconscious. I still didn't cry. Straightening up, I followed the nurse out the door and down the hall. Neither of us spoke, and I went back to my marathon walk in front of the nurses' station.

Three white dresses—her First Holy Communion, Graduation, and the Senior Prom. I couldn't shake the color out of my mind. And now a fourth white gown—not a wedding dress, but a hospital gown.

My mind jumped to another scene—destroying, turgid, devastating. It was Mother's Day two years ago. Jim was home, and as my present he was taking us out to dinner. Shirley had sent me a card with some flowers and I surprised them by giving Jim a boutonniere and Shirley a small corsage. It was in the early afternoon and we were getting dressed for the occasion.

In the morning I was very pleased when Jim told us of his plans, and was genuinely surprised. It was a beautiful Spring day.

About one o'clock, however, I said, "Jim, perhaps we better not go out for dinner."

"Why not, Mother? Don't worry about the money. I've been saving for this."

"It isn't that, but I'm afraid Shirley is taking something. She's not well. I can tell."

"I don't think so. She appears fine to me."

"All right. I'll go by your opinion and judgment. I was only concerned she might cause some embarrassment."

"Now Mother, I think you're being overly suspicious. Besides, it will be good for all three of us to get out of here for the day."

Perhaps Jim was right, and my fears were groundless. One of her doctors, I remembered, had told me to display a more positive attitude. Rather than preventing her from taking medication, I should place more trust and confidence in her.

I also knew it would be good if she left the apartment. The latter was a source of much difficulty. For about a year and a half prior to this incident, Shirley had been intermittently either at home or in Memorial Hospital. I, of course, worked every day, and if Shirley wasn't hospitalized she was home alone.

When I left the apartment in the morning, she would be in bed, and frequently was still there upon my return in the evening. Forty percent of the time, she never left her bed except to go to the bathroom or get something to eat. She called me at work three or four times most days, making up various excuses for her calls. For instance, she would say, "What do you want for dinner?" She had no one to talk to and was lonely.

Her voice was never crisp on the phone, so I surmised she was always taking medication. When she didn't call, it was a bad sign. I'd try to reach her, and sometimes she didn't answer. If she did, it was hard to understand her. Occasionally, the phone slipped out of her hands, and I would hear it striking the floor.

Then my mind conjured up different disasters—fire—damage through a bad fall to her head or leg again. This was bad enough, but when Jim left his car at home I could not relax all day. One half of my brain would be working at my job, and the other half would be sitting in the back seat of Jim's car, watching Shirley being questioned by the police, or shuddering as she hit some old lady in a crosswalk and drove off to escape the law. Thankfully, no trouble ever occurred.

She never saw anyone other than Jim and myself. No

matter how much we encouraged her to see her old friends again, in one way or another the proposed meetings never came to fruition. Even when someone was invited to the apartment, she would make a perfunctory appearance, then retire quickly, saying she wasn't feeling well.

The night we talked about going out to dinner, I hoped Jim's prognosis was right—that I was just being nervous for no reason—and that Shirley was fine. Even if she weren't completely well, going out together would convey to her our true desire to have her with us.

"Hi, Mum, you certainly look pretty in that dress. Is it the one Aunt Charlotte sent you?"

Before I could answer, she continued, "Here, let me pin on your corsage."

"I'd like that very much."

Shirley hadn't finished dressing; she was still in her slip. I was deeply concerned now that she was taking something; her speech was so rapid. Maybe she was excited about going out; I hoped so.

"Are you going to wear your black dress, Shirley? You know the one you wore to the Reese's for dinner?"

"I don't know. Maybe. I haven't decided."

Jim came in, all ready to go, and announced he was going for gas and to pick up the *New York Times.*

"I'll be back in half an hour. You be ready."

Shirley went in the bedroom to finish dressing, while I read the local paper.

Jim came back in high spirits, clapped his hands a couple of times, and quipped, "All right, girls, we're about to move out. Make sure you put that lipstick on straight. I'm only going out with pretty girls today."

He turned to me. "Mother, how about putting my boutonniere on for me?" As I was doing this, he called to

Shirley, "Hurry up, Shirley. I should have known better than to try to date two girls at once."

He was trying to make us feel as we did before our difficulties.

Shirley entered wearing a simple cotton sports dress.

"Oh, no, Shirley," I said. "You're not going to wear that dress. Why, I have reservations at the Trent-Hallstead."

Jim stopped abruptly. He'd been planning to surprise us.

Shirley muttered, "Why don't you two go? I'm not feeling well."

Jim's response was quick and determined. "Nothing doing. Go in and change your dress, and hurry up or we'll be late."

"I have a bad headache and I'm afraid I'll be sick," Shirley said.

"You can be sick with us, then," Jim retorted.

"All right." Shirley went slowly into the bedroom and shut the door.

Her attitude was a shock to both of us, as we'd all been in such good humor. Much as I hated to disappoint him, I suggested to Jim perhaps it would be best if he cancelled the reservations. But he was determined to continue with his plans, and remarked, "She isn't staying in this apartment alone today."

In a little while Shirley returned in her black dress. Jim held my coat, but when he tried to help Shirley into hers, she grabbed it from him and sat down on the sofa, staring at the floor.

There was no further doubt in my mind that she was taking medication. Yet she still had enough control to appear in public without others being aware of her condition. I was standing aside, watching both of them, and could see Jim's neck begin to bulge as the blood rushed to his head.

Fiercely, losing his temper momentarily, he seized Shirley's arm and jerked her to her feet. He yanked her coat, still keeping a tight grip on her arm. Shirley fought so violently to free herself, her hair became disheveled. My feet remained fixed, although I did manage to cry out, begging them to stop, and repeating several times, "It's Mother's Day."

Jim let go then, and throwing the coat in her face, shouted, "Put it on!"

"You can't make me do anything. And I'm going to stay here. I told you I don't feel too well."

"Oh, yeah. Well, you watch me. I'll put it on you."

And he did, somehow, pushing her towards the front door. She struggled, finally breaking away, and ran into the bathroom, locking the door, hysterical.

Jim was furious. "Come on, Mother. Let's go. Forget about her. I'll see you in the car."

He strode out of the apartment.

I stood there, unable to make a decision which way to turn, not knowing which child to uphold or comfort. Finally, noticing Shirley's corsage lying on the floor, I walked over and picked it up. It was crushed; it had been stepped on.

As I was holding it in my hands, Jim came in the door, put his arm around me, and said gently, "I'm sorry, Mother. Please don't be upset. Come on. Let's you and I go. It will do you good."

With little spring in our steps, we walked to the car.

The Trent-Hallstead was crowded, and I was extremely proud being with Jim as we were led to our table, and he seated me. While sipping our cocktails, I told Jim to order me turkey. Jokingly, but meaning it, he bantered, "Well, that's fine. I'm going to have oysters on the half shell, and I had planned to order Chateaubriand for us. But I'll change to a filet."

He laughed, and I went along with the mood. "Nothing

doing. We'll have Chateaubriand, but I'll have shrimp cocktail instead of the oysters."

"Oh, no you don't. You made your decision."

When the waiter came, he did order the Chateaubriand, and then a bottle of wine. I resolved to put $20 in his pocket that night.

We arrived home in the early evening, about seven o'clock. I betrayed my underlying anxiety by immediately calling Shirley's name as we came in the door. There was no answer. Jim went to the bedroom door, knocked lightly and called, "Shirley?"

Still no answer. Opening the door, he found the room empty. She had left.

"Is she asleep, Jim?" I asked.

"No, she's gone someplace. She isn't here."

"Where could she be, Jim? Maybe we'd better drive around and look for her."

"Why?" Jim remonstrated.

"Because I don't like her to be out alone when she's like this."

"She probably walked up to the drugstore for cigarettes. Please take off your coat, Mother, and sit down."

After an hour had passed, without saying anything to Jim, I went out to search for her. I drove to all the places I could possibly imagine she might have gone. Unsuccessful, I returned to the apartment.

"Is Shirley home, Jim?"

"What?" Jim asked as he looked up from the paper.

"Did Shirley come back?"

"No, she didn't."

"I'm getting worried. It's dark now."

"Perhaps I should call the drugstores, although most of them are closed now, I imagine."

Still no sign of her, and no one had seen her.

"Jim, why don't you call her father?"

"She wouldn't be out there."

"I don't think so either, but maybe she's contacted him."

"All right. How do I reach him?"

I gave Jim the number of the motel where he lived, and where he'd started working about a month before. Ted knew nothing, but he promised to call us at once if he received any word. The next two hours seemed endless. Even Jim became noticeably nervous.

At last the phone rang, and Jim answered it in the den. I stayed where I was, but could hear snatches of the long conversation and knew it concerned Shirley. Afterwards, Jim told me she was at Ted's motel. I could see he was reluctant to give me details, and it was only with persistent questioning I did learn this much. Shirley was in bad shape and had arrived with a young man in a taxi. Ted thought it wise for her to remain there for the night. He wanted to get rid of her companion, who was a most unsavory character and who had been drinking heavily.

Who could Shirley's date be? Was it someone she'd met tonight, or had she known him for some time? Thinking it over, I came to the conclusion she'd undoubtedly planned to meet him. That was why she didn't want to go with us today, and why she'd put on the sports dress. I mentioned this to Jim and he agreed. He remarked, "Remember, how she'd say she was kept waiting at the doctor's—never a quick visit anyplace? Now it doesn't take three, five, and once I remember nine hours to see a doctor. I'll bet she's been meeting this man for some time."

One reason why Jim and I never suspected she was seeing any men was because she was never out late at night, and spent the majority of her time at home.

Knowing where she was relieved us somewhat, and despite the new development, Jim insisted we try to get some sleep.

"I'll go out early in the morning, and bring her back."

Very early the next morning, Jim left to pick up Shirley. I remained at home. When they returned, she said nothing and immediately went to bed. Jim was extremely uncommunicative. I never did learn the entire story, but did manage to find out a little of what had happened.

Apparently, upon her arrival at the motel, Ted gave Shirley a room and advised the young man with her to leave. Some words passed between them but the stranger did finally go. However, about two hours later, Ted went up to Shirley's room to be sure she was all right. To Ted's surprise, he found the stranger in her room. A violent scene ensued which culminated in the arrival of the police and in the boy's subsequent arrest. I later found out that he had a police record in two or three different states.

The memories of the experiences of that Mother's Day would never leave me. Going from a normal even life to cataclysmic bolts of sordidness. I shuddered.

How was I to judge the strength of Shirley's will in thwarting her addictive drive, after so many years of emotional and physical suffering? I thought about this night, which might well be her last. She was to be pitied. For her to take such an excess of drugs, not meaning to destroy herself, and yet to become enmeshed in a web of self-destruction, like a fly stalked by a spider in his web, was really sad. She was caught, and couldn't seem to find an opening to escape.

I'm not denying Shirley couldn't make some kind of a choice, but as to her culpability, I couldn't judge. After all, she began by taking medication under the express orders of a physician, and always followed directions given her very carefully. She didn't begin for pleasure or as an escape mechanism, but eventually her system demanded medication in ever-increasing amounts. She was wrong, she was guilty of an insatiable appetite, and was aware of her excesses.

I prayed silently,

"Please, God, if Shirley survives, somehow—somehow, help her to find the way out of this labyrinth."

CHAPTER 11

"Mrs. Daniels," I felt a hand on my shoulder. "I'm sorry to wake you."

"Oh, you didn't wake me. I was thinking—going over some things in my mind—in a world of my own, I guess."

"I wanted to give you these; they'll be safer in your purse, Mrs. Daniels." I looked; three articles in all. Shirley's watch, Shirley's bracelet, Shirley's medal. I held them in my hand for a few minutes and stared at them. Then I read the notation on the back of the watch, "To Shirley on your Graduation Day from Mother and Dad."

I placed them in my purse and looked into space. Temporarily, I wished my mind and brain would cease functioning, but this was an impossibility. Instead, they continued to produce fresh images from yesterday, all of them sad. Not every incident which passed through my mind had been an unhappy one at the time. Quite the contrary. It was tonight's tragedy which tinged everything with sadness, even the most joyful and happy events of the past.

Why didn't I cry? I asked myself this from far away. It would have been natural to do so. Too much had transpired during the preceding 15 hours. I might have cried in the beginning when my emotions had too much energy to control. But in the beginning, I had had so much to do. In order to resolve the problem in some way, I had to be completely alert. In truth there hadn't been time to cry—no time when I could have permitted my feelings to hold sway.

Now the doctors and nurses had taken over. The hospital was responsible for Shirley. I couldn't pick up the end tables; I couldn't stop her from falling; I couldn't care for her in any way. I could only sit and wait. Yet no tears fell or needed to be wiped away, for my emotions were as exhausted as I.

The hospital personnel were very kind, and most anxious that I try and rest. An empty but thoughtful gesture! My daughter's life might be ending. How could I rest? Maybe I should have put my feet up, but I didn't.

Being tired was a blessing, for it made Shirley's crisis easier for me to endure. Had I been fully rested, my mind and reactions would not have been numbed, and hysteria might have reigned. Or maybe it might have been better for me if I had cracked wide open. But I didn't crack.

Drugs are not choosers of people. A funny phrase, maybe, but it entered my mind during that long night. I used to feel ashamed and embarrassed to admit Shirley was caught by this horrible addiction—caught with all those insidious little pills. I wouldn't admit a vise so strong had so firmly gripped my daughter. For a long time, unconsciously perhaps, I refused to believe the evidence which played out before my eyes. I turned away, literally closing my eyes to the entire problem and its resulting situations.

Two of the girls with whom I worked had returned from their lunch hour one day and casually mentioned they'd seen Shirley in a nearby drugstore. I laughed and informed them this was an impossibility as Shirley was home sick in bed. Mickey was not swayed, "Oh, no. It was Shirley all right. She was getting a prescription while I was buying some stockings. I'm sure it was she, because of her leg."

I proceeded in all sincerity to convince them they'd been mistaken. Had I only perceived the obvious at an earlier date? But then does anyone really convince themselves about the faults of someone they love until it is too late? Very seldom.

"Mrs. Daniels." My reverie was broken, and I got up from the chair. "Yes?"

"Please don't get up." It was the nurse, Miss Brevoort. "Is anyone coming to the hospital to be with you at this time?"

I guess she assumed someone was on their way to be with me. "No. I don't expect anyone. My son may arrive in the morning if she is still critically ill."

"Isn't there someone you could get to be with you right now?"

"I'm here. It's my daughter. I'm afraid no one else will be here."

I spoke very sharply. Her father's disinterest and utter lack of feeling and love shocked and hurt me for her sake. I was the sole witness to her birth, and apparently was to play the same role at her death. But immediately I added, "I'm sorry. I didn't mean to be so short, Miss Brevoort. I'm a little upset."

"That's all right, Mrs. Daniels. I understand. However, we don't like anyone to be alone at a time like this."

The knife in my heart, which had been there all day and night was brutally turned 90 degrees. She was telling me as gently as possible they didn't think Shirley would live.

I attempted to compose my thoughts. "I'll call someone, Miss Brevoort, and ask them to come. Thank you for your kindness and please forgive my rudeness."

Whom to call? Whom to call? I began thinking of different friends. Which one would I want close to me at this time and under these circumstances? Every name which popped into my mind had some reservations connected with it. They weren't close enough to me; their husbands weren't sympathetic to the problem, and wouldn't relish a phone call so late at night, much less having to go out in the cold at this hour; they lived too far away. There wasn't anyone I could think of.

My brothers and sisters lived in the Middle West. If only George could come, but he couldn't. Strangely, I didn't want some people to know about it. If Shirley recovered I wanted to save her from any further embarrassment. This was silly, for she wouldn't be here much longer anyway.

Whom should I call? Slowly, I'd been moving towards the telephone booth, and found myself inside at last, fumbling through my purse, looking for a dime. No dime. Absent-mindedly, I pulled down the coin return and saw one. What luck! It had been there since I'd phoned Jim and charged the call to my own number.

Still in a half-daze, I put the 10 cents in the slot, listened for the dial tone and dialed. I came to when I heard the telephone ringing at the other end of the line. It rang and rang and rang. It never occurred to me I didn't know who it was I had called. Finally, an answer. "Hello."

A man was speaking sleepily.

"Who is this, please?" I asked, in a small voice.

"Lady, I believe you called me. If you don't wish to identify yourself, then goodnight."

"Wait!" I almost screamed. "This is Mary Daniels."

"Mary." The voice was no longer sleepy. "What's the matter? Has something happened?"

I recognized the voice, and obviously he was a good friend of mine, but I was still unable to place it. "Who is this," I finally queried again.

"Why, Mary, this is Dave Regan. What's the matter?"

"Oh, Dave." I was so relieved.

The Regans' name had never come into my mind. What subconscious force had moved my fingers, I would never know. I must have been speaking more rapidly than usual, because several times Dave asked me to slow down and repeat. I explained the situation, trying to be calm and explicit.

"Dave," I added at the conclusion, "The nurses feel I should have someone with me and I wondered if Carol would come and spend even a short time?"

"I'm sorry, Mary. So very sorry to hear of all this trouble."

"Could I speak to Carol and ask her, Dave?"

"That won't be necessary. Carol will be right over, Mary. I'll wake her and tell her immediately. She'll be there as soon as possible."

"Dave. If you think it will be too much for her, please don't call her."

"Nonsense. Hang up. She'll arrive in 20 minutes to half-an-hour, I'd say. What floor is Shirley on, Mary?"

"She's on the fourth, Dave. In the Intensive Care Unit—now, if you feel. . . ." He hung up before I finished the sentence.

Dave and Carol lived only a short distance from the hospital. They had experienced much difficulty in their own lives, and consequently had the depth of understanding I needed. Also, Carol had a small car. Thus, Dave wouldn't have to come, nor would he be stranded without transportation should this prove to be a long vigil.

Carol wouldn't talk too much or be overly sympathetic. I couldn't have chosen a better person for support. We would be able to talk calmly, for some of the problems Carol had faced in her own life had given her an innate understanding and the right amount of common sense.

". . . but we don't like anyone to be alone at a time like this." The words of the nurse kept repeating themselves in my mind.

I knew what she meant. The end was near. Shirley didn't have a chance; she wouldn't survive the night; she had lived her last day; she wouldn't breathe any more. What a long, long road it had been from her babyhood to this night. She would never cry again, never smile again.

". . . but we don't like anyone to be alone at a time like this."

Nothing functioned now beyond my thoughts of Shirley. Maybe it would be better if she died. Her life had not been happy during the past several years. So much pain and physical suffering.

Shirley had been gifted in languages, and had intended to major in French at college and go abroad for her Junior year. France's Unknown Soldier never received her visit; the falling snow at Winter Carnival never dusted her hair; nor were her lips ever caressed by any young college man.

When my Aunt Susan died of cancer some years ago, we all commented it was the best thing because of her suffering. But this wasn't my aunt. This was Shirley, my daughter. I couldn't say whether it would be better for her to be taken or not. I wanted her to live, but not to suffer like this the rest of her life.

Back and forth, back and forth. With slow measured steps I continued my pacing. Suddenly I stood still, frozen. Where would I bury her? We didn't own a cemetery lot. I had no place. What church would I use? I wasn't even acquainted with the pastor of my new parish. I wouldn't be known there. Would many people be at the funeral? Probably not, for Shirley had lost all contact with her friends since her illness had begun. I had no place for her to be buried. The thought kept hammering at me.

I'd often heard people say jokingly at cocktail parties, "Well, when I'm dead, I'm dead. Take me right out in the basket—no coffin, please."

I recalled, too, the discussions about cremation—the

pros and cons, and how people had willed their ashes to be scattered over some area of the world. I even might have made such a remark myself, half-believing, half-joking. But tonight was a different story. I didn't want Shirley to be buried anywhere alone. I wished her to be near someone who was kind and gentle, so at least in death she might know warmth, understanding and security. Where would I bury her? Then, as so frequently during the long hours of waiting, the face of my mother came before me. I felt better at once, for I knew the answer. Next to my mother. And Shirley would rest peacefully there. I knew it. I felt it. It was a great relief, and a tremendous strain was lifted from me.

I was about 30 feet from the elevator when the door opened. It was Carol. She didn't see me and began to walk away from me towards the nurses' station, so I called, "Carol. Carol."

She turned, hurried towards me and threw her arms around me. Neither of us could speak. With Carol's arrival, I had a feeling of complete weakness—almost a collapse. My legs must have sagged for she assisted me at once to a bench in the hall. Instead of becoming stronger with Carol's companionship, and her added support, I was drained of my previous strength.

At last I spoke. "Shirley is very sick—very bad, Carol."

"I know, Mary. I'm so very sorry."

"Thank you for coming."

"You should have called me earlier, Mary."

"I didn't want to bother you—didn't really want to bother anyone. Finally, the nurse told me they preferred my not being alone at this time." I paused to gain control of my voice. "It's critical. They gave me her watch, bracelet and medal."

"Do you want to tell me about it, Mary?"

"Well, I'd picked Shirley up at the State Hospital this morning. She'd been given permission to remain at home until today. . . ." It took me 10 or 15 minutes to give Carol a brief resume of the preceding hours of our day.

By the time I finished she was crying quietly, and I was comforting her. Carol kept saying, "Why didn't you call me, Mary?"

I found myself asking Carol about her family—were they well, and how was her recently married daughter getting along? The latter had been one of Shirley's close friends, and on occasion had tried to help her.

In some ways it was more difficult for me now that Carol was there. I was thankful and more than grateful for her company, but I felt I had to say something at times, although I wished to remain silent.

We were still sitting on the bench when Miss Brevoort approached us. "Mrs. Daniels?"

Carol and I rose simultaneously. "Miss Brevoort, this is Mrs. Regan."

"Hello, Mrs. Regan. I'm so glad you could come over. Mrs. Daniels has been alone too long."

"Had I only known, I would have been here sooner."

"Mrs. Daniels. Why don't you and Mrs. Regan go out on the sun porch? There's a couch out there where you could lie down for a little while. Even if you can't sleep, you'll be able to rest."

"I don't know if I could lie down."

"Please try." Miss Brevoort was most concerned, I could see.

"Yes, Mary," Carol was firm. "We should try, anyway."

She took me by one arm, and Miss Brevoort by the other, and we proceeded to the couch on the sun porch. I stretched out as best I could, and Carol pulled a chair alongside of me. I closed my eyes and felt a blanket being placed over me.

"Mrs. Daniels." Miss Brevoort had a glass of water in one hand, and a small paper cup in the other. "Your doctor called and wants you to take this pill. It will help you rest."

A pill. It was too much for me even to think about. "Thank you, Miss Brevoort. I appreciate your interest and my doctor's, but I can't take the pill."

"Please, Mrs. Daniels. It is the mildest type of sedative, and can't possibly hurt you. The doctor feels strongly about this."

"I'm sorry, Miss Brevoort, I never want to see or even hear about another sedative or sleeping pill. I simply can't face it."

I did drink the glass of water, though, and again closed my eyes. I didn't sleep. How could I? Shirley was dying from an overdose of medication and alcohol. The thought kept plaguing me that it might be better for her to die. Then, like an attack of ague, the horrible realization came over me. I was wishing for my daughter to die. "I didn't mean that," I would say to myself.

But what kind of life did Shirley have to look forward to? I had read enough and talked to many doctors and knew her chances were extremely small in overcoming an addiction problem. Particularly since it was coupled with her constantly recurring physical difficulties.

Lying there, my mind was literally torn between the living and the dead. Occasionally, I made an effort to tear myself free from these morbid thoughts, and I would remember Carol and talk with her. Finally, my thoughts overflowed and I had to tell her what was upsetting me.

"Try not to think of the past, Mary. Don't worry about it now. Remember, every road is straight but it always comes to a curve. Whether it will turn to the left or right we never know until it is reached. So it won't do any good to get upset until we reach the curve in Shirley's road."

It was good advice, but I couldn't accept it. For years I had tried every possible solution to her problem. None had worked. Kindness, sternness, cajoling, flattery, appealing to Shirley's pride—all had failed. Each new defeat produced a wilder and more radical answer.

I was like a student learning algebra for the first time, a student who had no aptitude for mathematics. In the early part of the course I would have more right answers than wrong. As the difficulties increased, the wrong problems outnumbered the right ones. Studying harder failed to produce anything positive. All my homework papers were progressively worse. Finally, I ceased doing them, but still took the examinations. I would hope for a miracle to give me all the answers without having any knowledge of the material covered. When this didn't materialize I wanted to withdraw, for to remain meant failure. But I couldn't withdraw so the outcome was inevitable. Then for the rest of the course, I would be like another desk in the classroom, never contributing, never trying—a piece of furniture, resigned to disaster.

This was the way my life had been running. My fight was gone. I had just about lost hope, and maybe my daughter's failure would be erased by death.

Who had been wrong? Shirley, I, or the doctors? Perhaps all three. I had first tried to help Shirley by taking her to various specialists, and refused in my own mind to believe anything like drug addiction could occur to anyone in my family. Even when I gave in slightly, and let myself become partially aware of the dimensions of the problem, I was still convinced in my heart there was a way out because it was my firm belief every problem had a solution. Wasn't there an answer for every math problem in the textbook? Only there it was simplified—all I had to do was turn to the back of the book.

She was sick, but no medical solution could determine her illness. Otherwise she would have been cured by surgery, treatment or medicine. I had found her problem could not be resolved in such a neat fashion.

On many occasions I had taken her by ambulance to the hospital. Often, she was retching and vomiting blood. Some organic ailments would be found, but with intravenous feedings and intensive care, within a week or two she would begin to look like her old self.

The doctors and I thought her frequent illnesses were connected with the many infections she had had after her leg operations.

Within a few days following her release, the old pattern would be resumed. Thus, I had learned a physical withdrawal could be effected. It never lasted because she had never made a mental withdrawal. Self-denial, I felt, had to be the answer to Shirley's problem.

But this was the frustrating puzzle. How could Shirley literally be "cornered" into an avenue of health and a happy life again? I tried every approach, even fear. She would respond favorably for a few days, then fall again, and I was never able to build a desire strong enough for physical well-being and a normal life, which could permanently blunt her overwhelming desire for drugs.

One of her psychiatrists used a mild type of pill in an attempt to have Shirley achieve a degree of balance, and to lessen her nervousness. This treatment was successful for a time. He had told her she would continue on the medication for the rest of her life.

When I learned this, I knew it would fail, for he was simply making a physical substitute rather than effecting a complete reversal of mental attitude. He was making Shirley a legalized addict.

I was furious. He wanted Shirley to live the rest of her life without complete freedom. He was treating her somewhat like a diabetic. A diabetic had to be dependent upon insulin; Shirley would have to be dependent upon drugs. But there I felt the similarity ended. Insulin brought a diabetic's body into chemical balance, but drugs would keep Shirley's system permanently awry. In addition, I had never heard of an addict who did not increase his consumption continuously. I had quite an argument with the psychiatrist concerning his prognosis.

At first I listened patiently when he explained his reasons for treating her with the pill. I told him, however, I didn't agree, and explained I thought medicine and its ally, psychiatry, should, if at all possible, place Shirley back into the aura of health she had enjoyed before her illness.

From then on we were permanently at odds, and I never saw him again. In fact, of late I hadn't spoken to any of the doctors. It was always I, the lay person, versus the technically competent. I could never walk in and discuss Shirley on an equal basis. If this had occurred, I would have been able to point out every treatment which failed. I couldn't understand pursuing the same paths again. A new method had to be used. The most logical one, which amazingly had never been employed, was the use of medical advice and encouragement so Shirley could eventually stand alone.

The nurse came in again. "Hello, Mrs. Regan. Is she asleep?"

"I believe so," answered Carol.

I heard the voices as if from a long distance away. "What is it, Miss Brevoort?" I sat up straight.

"I've some encouraging news, Mrs. Daniels. It's very little, so don't get your hopes up too high."

Carol and I literally held our breaths as she continued, "We have finally obtained a reaction from Shirley. It's the first favorable indication since she came into the hospital. I want you to understand, though, she is not out of danger."

And Miss Brevoort was gone.

A sense of weightlessness swirled within my head. It seemed to pull me up off the couch, and I had the feeling if I didn't get up, my head would detach itself and rise to the clouds like a balloon filled with helium.

Carol took my hand and held it tightly. At last she spoke, "There, Mary. I told you things would be better."

"Well, Carol, we're not out of the woods yet—not by a long shot, I know."

"No, I guess not. But at least we have an inkling of hope."

It was true. A little bit of hope had nourished my mind and spirit for a long time. Whenever I could see just a glimmer, I could always continue marching forward. Without it, I found the abyss of depression had no bottom. One little ray, the smallest ray of hope which could be measured, always gave me strength, perhaps not to move mountains, but at least to continue to fight. "The thing which frightens me, Carol, is even if Shirley manages to pull through, she won't escape without brain damage. She's been unconscious, and her circulation has been bad for so many hours."

"Try not to think of it, Mary. You can only manage one thing at a time. How can you or anyone know what will happen? We have to believe things will remain as they were until proven otherwise."

Please God, if Shirley should make it tonight, let her have a chance at getting better in every way. It wasn't fair to send trouble to her always. She had had enough, far more than her share. Let her be allowed to walk in peace for at least a little while.

I realized she had many happy times as a youngster, perhaps a far better youth than most children, for we had some money in those days and lived a very comfortable life. And Shirley had always responded by working very hard, both in school and at home.

Her illnesses had all been too much for anyone to bear. The pressure had been on for too long a period of time, and at too great a rate. There had to be a breaking point. How much longer—how much longer could it all go on?

CHAPTER 12

"WOULDN'T YOU ENJOY a cup of coffee, Mary?"

"Fine, Carol. I'd love one. There's a machine on the first floor." We decided to walk down together.

At the elevator, we were hailed by Dr. Turner, who wished to speak to me alone. "May I speak to you for a minute privately, please, Mrs. Daniels?"

"Yes, doctor. But you may talk freely in front of Mrs. Regan. She's completely familiar with Shirley's case."

"Well, Mrs. Daniels, as Miss Brevoort told you, we have succeeded in obtaining a small favorable reaction from Shirley. Her chances of recovery are increasing. We feel the percentages are in her favor now. I must tell you, however, this was very critical and serious. For a long while we had no hope whatsoever. As a matter of fact, we were just about ready to perform a tracheotomy. She is still not completely out of danger, but it does look promising."

"Thank you so much, Dr. Turner. You and all the staff have been most kind. I am most grateful."

"We're happy, too. You've been very brave. We all admire you." Dr. Turner left and I turned to Carol. I felt utterly drained of all energy.

"Oh, Carol, I think I'm going to cry." And I placed my head on her shoulder.

"There, there, Mary. It's going to be all right."

The first lights of a new day were coming through the windows of the sun porch. It was also another dawn for Shirley.

"Carol, I'll be all right. I don't mind being alone now. I won't leave anyway until I can go back and see Shirley, and it may be a few hours. Why don't you go home and get some rest?"

"It's too soon, Mary. Let's wait together for a little while longer. I'm going to call Dave and let him know how things are going."

I could see no amount of argument would persuade Carol to leave, so when she returned I stretched out again and pulled the blanket up over my shoulders. Utter exhaustion had finally come over me. "Perhaps I could sleep now, Carol."

And sleep I did. When I awoke, I saw Carol was again sitting in the chair next to me. "How long did I sleep?" I asked.

"Only about 40 minutes, I'm sorry to say. I was hoping you'd be able to get a good hour or longer. Do you feel any better?"

"I think I must, or I'd never have been able to rest."

It was now morning, which reminded me, "Oh, Carol. What about Dave? I forgot to ask you. What did he say? You did talk to him?"

"Oh, yes. But he told me not to rush home, just to take my time. Don't worry about Dave. He knows how to cook his breakfast."

"He's a wonderful man, Carol. A real friend."

I was beginning to feel better, and was able to fill Carol in on some of the details of the past 24 hours. However, I couldn't bring myself to relate how Ted had refused to come to the hospital, and how he had left me alone. I don't know why I withheld his role, but I suppose I was ashamed, not of him, necessarily, but perhaps of myself. I hated to admit I had married such a spineless individual, a man who couldn't be a father to his own child even at her moment of death. Maybe I hated to face up to it—to admit my judgment had been so terribly warped and wrong.

After I finished my story, Carol sensed I had no more to tell, so she picked up a magazine and leafed through the pages. I walked over to the window and looked out.

In a few minutes Miss Brevoort came through the French doors, her face happy with a warm smile. "Mrs. Daniels. Shirley is off the critical list and is responding well. Most encouraging of all, she has attempted to speak."

"Oh, thank you for coming to tell us, Miss Brevoort. You've been wonderful."

She hurriedly departed and I walked back to Carol. "Carol, you really must be on your way. I won't take a refusal again now that she's better."

"All right, Mary. If you're sure. But when do you think you'll leave yourself to go home and get some rest? Goodness knows, you could use it more than I."

"Soon, Carol. I'd like to see Shirley before I go. It would make me happier to know myself she's better, even though I can't make any medical judgment."

Carol had her hat and coat on, and was waiting for the elevator. I decided to go with her to her car, and asked her to wait.

"Oh, never mind, Mary."

"The air will do me good, Carol."

After she had driven away, I walked around the block, which encompassed the hospital, taking in deep breaths of the cold morning air.

One minute I was looking up the empty street, and the next I found myself staring at the sky. I had slipped on a patch of ice. Obviously, I wasn't hurt, and I laughed aloud sitting alone on the sidewalk. I'd be in the emergency ward next if I wasn't careful.

Noticing a small diner close by, I went over to get toast and coffee. Two or three truck drivers were having breakfast. They all turned and looked at me.

I realized they must have thought I'd been on an all-night binge—because of the way I looked—and I had been, but on a different type than they envisaged.

I couldn't stop giggling when I picked up my cup, for my hand was shaking, spilling the coffee, and the men stared at me again.

Before I left, I smiled at all of them, probably confirming their suspicions I wasn't completely sane. And maybe I wasn't right at that moment. I didn't know nor did I care.

I was experiencing a big emotional let-down after Shirley's crisis. As long as the outcome had remained in doubt, my mind had rushed from one corner to another. My physical movements exhibited the same briskness. Of course Shirley was never helped by my increased activity, but I suppose it aided me. If I had had to remain still, my system would have cracked. I was reminded of a friend who had been in the Army, and who thought its motto should be, "Hurry up and wait." It could well have been my slogan with Shirley, plus the added ingredient—fear.

Miss Brevoort came to bid me farewell. She had her hat and coat on. "I'm going off duty now, and wanted to say goodbye and wish you the best of luck in the future—to Shirley, too, but particularly to you, Mrs. Daniels." She put her arms around me for a moment.

"Thank you, Miss Brevoort, for everything."

"Shirley is going to get better now, I feel sure. What else will happen we have no way of knowing. Please take care of yourself, Mrs. Daniels. I know how hard it is not to worry, but we don't want you to be sick, too."

We exchanged goodbyes. I would really miss her and thought, to myself, "Miss Brevoort is on her way to a warm home and I hope a good restful sleep." I tried not to feel sorry for myself, and only to remember how wonderful she had been. I hoped everything in her life was happy and normal.

The hospital was beginning to stir—beginning to wake up. Morning had definitely arrived. I'd always noticed its daily existence was divided into two phases, night and day. The activity at night was muted, rather like a person trying to sleep with no success. By morning, the effort to rest was given up, shrugged off, and with the determination sleep couldn't be obtained, work was resumed with all the hustle and bustle that could be mustered.

Nurses, aides, and interns were hurrying someplace, all pictures of diligence. People walked past me. Some stared; some didn't notice. I must have looked worn and bedraggled, and I surmised the hospital personnel wondered what I was doing there so early in the morning. Some probably thought my husband had had a heart attack, or that there had been an accident in the family. Others had probably given up long ago trying to figure out why I or any person would be in the hospital at this hour.

I was sure the new shift would now be discussing Shirley and me. I didn't care. Tired, completely enervated, I was like a mechanical sack of straw trained to move on certain given signals. The smile indicator was set into motion by anyone who came into view. My lips stretched, and parted slightly, attempting to turn upwards; my head nodded once or twice and turned in unison with the person. When he disappeared,

I reverted to the limp straw woman. Nothing registered inside me; nothing was imprinted on my mind. Undoubtedly, if someone had said "boo," I would have smiled.

I vaguely noticed a strange nurse had come up to me. "You may go back and see your daughter now, for 15 minutes only. I must tell you she won't know you or remember anything, but don't be upset about this. Afterwards you should go home and rest. She's going to be moved out of Intensive Care in a few hours, and there's no danger in your leaving. She's going to be all right."

"I'd like very much to see her. Thank you."

After escorting me to Shirley, the nurse left immediately, and I was alone with my only daughter. She was strapped into the bed, to prevent as little movement as possible, yet was writhing and attempting to mumble through her thickened lips. She was being fed intravenously and still had various tubes in her.

I could distinguish no articulation at all, and wondered if by any chance she was trying to enunciate my name. There was no way then, or ever, I would know.

Her movements were very intense and determined. She looked absolutely awful. In addition to the thickness and swelling of her mouth, her face was bloated. The whole scene became unreal to me. Her distorted expression, the color of her bleached hair, gave her an almost macabre appearance.

Shirley, Shirley—where were we headed? What was going to happen? After a few minutes I went over to the bed and took hold of her hand as best I could between all the strappings and tubes. I spoke to her quietly, but nothing registered with her, I'm sure. All the time in my own heart I was silently praying. I asked God to let her rise out of the pit in which she was ensnared.

All too soon the nurse came and led me out. "The time for your visit is up."

"That's all right," I replied. In one way I was glad it was over. There wasn't anything I could do now for Shirley, much as I hated to leave her. It was hard for me to see her in this dreadful condition.

I began to get ready to leave, and the nurse suggested I call in the afternoon. If Shirley was conscious I could return and talk to her. I had started to the elevator when the telephone rang at the Nurses' Station. The nurse motioned to me.

"This is Ann. How is Shirley, and how are you?"

"Shirley's better. She responded about two hours ago, and I saw her a few minutes ago. I just left her room now."

"I'm so glad, Mary, things seem somewhat better."

"I want to thank you and Ben again for last night. We would have been lost without you." It all seemed so long ago. I wondered for a moment if it had all really happened.

"Please, Mary. Don't thank us. That's what friends are for. What are you going to do now? Are you staying at the hospital?"

"No, I'm leaving right now to go home and try to sleep."

"Please, Mary, won't you come over here? I don't think you should go back to the apartment alone. It will be quiet at our house and Ben and I will see you get some rest. Please come."

I hadn't thought of returning home and picturing the scene of the whole dreadful chain of events. I hesitated. Perhaps it would be better if I didn't try to face it until after I had rested. "If you're sure it won't be any trouble, Ann, I'll come. Thank you."

"Fine, Mary. I'll get your bed ready."

As I hung up the phone, I was informed Dr. Deiss wanted to talk to me before I left the hospital. I was directed to an office. Two doctors were there. I recognized both of them as having been in attendance with Shirley the night before.

Dr. Deiss came straight to the point. "Mrs. Daniels," he said. "We are going to have to chart Shirley as an attempted suicide."

"Doctor," I queried. "Why would you say that?"

"Well, she's been in the State Hospital for some time, and we feel after being home with you today she couldn't face the thought of returning there."

I was staggered. "I disagree with you, doctor. I know Shirley took too much medication. The overdose occurred because she lost mental balance. She had no idea how much she had taken, and probably consumed pills like Life Savers."

"I think you're wrong, Mrs. Daniels. She will have to be charted as attempted suicide."

I thought for a second, *what difference would it make how they list her?* Then I realized this listing would be the basis for her future treatment.

"Now listen, doctor. That is simply not true. You have no reason for reaching your conclusion."

"Mrs. Daniels. We've had far more experience in these matters than you, and all the information we have received from both you and the authorities at the State Hospital lead us to this diagnosis."

"Don't you think I've had experience with this type of problem, doctor? After all, I'm the one who lives with and who has lived with this problem of Shirley's. Have you ever personally had anyone in your household who was an addict, or who has had Shirley's physical problems?"

I was vehemently angry, and raised my voice far above normal. The other doctor stepped into the argument and said, soothingly, "Now, Mrs. Daniels. Patients tell their doctors more than they tell their own families. You must at least give us credit for some professional competency."

Professional competency. He would only believe what he wished to believe, anyway. My opinion counted for little or nothing, and they would win in the end.

Disgusted, I arose, and said I had to leave.

I knew one thing, though. The doctors were wrong about last night, but for the next several days they would have to be careful with her. Now, if at any time, would be the suicidal time for Shirley. As soon as she began to come out of it and realized where she was and what had happened, and above all that she must return to the State Hospital and God knows what treatment, she would be completely depressed and at the same time wild at everyone. Completely frustrated in her own weak folly, she would, underneath, be most furious at herself. Now would be the time when she might easily attempt to take her own life. She was a potential suicide.

The cold morning air was refreshing as I walked to my car. I was soon well on my way to Ann and Ben's. Driving slowly, I wondered where it would all lead. What would I do now? What would Shirley do? How could this problem be resolved?

My family. What had happened to our life—all the roots I'd tried to establish—the traditions and niceties of living I had established despite the complete lack of father and husband?

Would we, Jim, Shirley and I, ever get off the ground again? Would we ever have a semblance of pleasant sailing? Or would the waters always be stormy, and apparent calm be, in reality, a calm before the storm? Perhaps periods of tranquility and order might lengthen by degrees and eventually replace the strains our bodies and spirits had endured these past many years.

How soon would an ambulance come to our door in the middle of the night? When would I have to ride with her again accompanied by the wail of sirens through the black night? I hadn't been able to prevent what happened this past night; or to halt any of the events or episodes leading up to it. So why shouldn't I give up? Why keep fighting? For what purpose had I been born? To try, and then fail and fail again?

The weights on both mind and body had become heavier. The millstone had ground smaller. My body was no longer able to support the old spirit and lilt.

Herein lay my greatest danger. It was to be the biggest fight of all, and had been in the past. I had to overcome the dictator of depression. It was the prison from which I had to escape.

I realized what faced me in the present, and what had bogged me down for many years before, for I was caught within the imprisonment of Shirley's affliction as I had been caught before with Ted's. Would there ever be any release, any answer for me? How old would I be if and when Shirley was cured? I'd never know—never with certainty. Would I be young enough to enjoy life if perchance fortune smiled upon me briefly during the span left of my life? I didn't know. Would death find me trapped in a jail not of my own doing nor of my own making? I didn't know. What was justice? Certainly not a part of this world nor of its occupants.

The only weapon with which I could keep fighting had been hope, for without hope I knew there was no chance—no chance for myself or for Shirley. If I gave up, she would be a ward of the State for the rest of her life. I was positive in my mind this was so. Shirley's recovery hinged on my survival.

She needed to be nourished in order to get well, and I believed the nourishment for anyone's problems was love— love based on complete faith and trust, and the joy of being loved in return. The source of Shirley's strength to fight her problem had to be this. I was sure. But was I capable of providing enough for her?

The drive was coming to an end.

"I must never give up. I must never give up. I must never give up." Without realizing it, I found I was repeating the phrase out loud.

But would it matter whether I continued to hope? Would it matter to Shirley or to anyone? Maybe she required more love now than I had left to give. Maybe she had passed the point where love meant anything to her.

"I must never give up. I must never give up. I must never give up." I was like the small boy or little girl now in class writing on the blackboard, "I will never talk again in class."

I found myself turning into Ann and Ben's driveway.

As I did, I heard the phrase again. "I must never give up."

AFTERWORD

MEMORY CAN BE a fleeting thing. But not always. Some memories never fade.

Though more than 70 years later, I can still see my mother's hands and fingers traversing the piano keys fluidly and effortlessly, almost miraculously, creating beautiful music, whether a classical concerto or a song she'd never heard before picked up by ear from hearing someone hum a few bars.

I see her on the 18th hole of our local golf course, needing to sink a final putt to win the club championship. Me, holding my breath. She made it.

I see my sister, Elizabeth, building sand castles with me on the beach on the New Jersey Shore, hoping they would still be there the next morning. I see her graduating from high school in a white dress, the prettiest girl in the class.

I see my father taking me to the local movie theater. He had just come home from work in the middle of a summer day after learning that our dog, Blitzen, had been killed on the street in the front of our house. I saw it happen. I see him reeling a record-setting channel bass after an hour-long fight, me worrying that the fish might pull him into the ocean.

Some memories never fade.

I suppose everyone's life is marked by periods of dark

tragedy. The story told in this book written by my mother brings back memories from the greatest tragedy in my life, and it sheds light on it that I never saw before.

This is probably the most *personally* moving and sobering book I have ever read. It was written by my mother about 50 years ago. I don't know the exact date, but she probably wrote it sometime between 1964, shortly after I joined P&G, and 1968. As an author-friend of hers wrote after reading it, "This is a terrifying book. If Aristotle's inelegant analogy 'catharsis' has any meaning or value, this book makes that meaning and value clear. It has an almost Greek beauty to it." That sums it up well.

The book tells a story that encompasses less than 24 hours during which my sister Elizabeth was allowed to come home from the state hospital where she was being treated for drug addiction.

Through her moving and cinema-like narrative, my mother provides a deeply and sorrowfully-etched description of what happened that day. In doing so, she reveals in the most transparent human way possible her relationships with my sister, my father, several of her friends and, in a small way, almost as an aside, me. I'm Jim in the story.

Through this agonizing tale, my mother's courage emerges strong and true. So does her willingness never to lose hope and never to give up.

I did not know my mother had written this until 2-3 years ago when the manuscript emerged from an unexamined random box which we had brought home after she passed away in 1975. I never recall my mother mentioning it. She appears to have spent some time trying to have it published, without success. I am publishing it now. Quite apart from its significance in my family's life, this is a story which I believe should be told because it speaks to a challenge which countless families are facing today in trying to help a family member or a friend overcome drug or alcohol addiction.

I grew up slowly but surely learning that my father was an alcoholic and that his alcoholism was ruining his and my mother's marriage. I can't recall at exactly what age I became aware of this unfolding tragedy. Certainly by the time I was eleven, the consequences were becoming more and more apparent and more acute. I experienced what a ravaging sickness alcoholism is, for the individual and for his or her family. It was terribly difficult for my mother and terribly unsettling for me and my sister. There were nights when I could see that my father was being taken to a recovery center. I could see that my parents' marriage was crumbling. Still, even through the turmoil, my parents were creating an environment that showed how much they valued education and how much they cared about me and my sister.

My mother was the brightest of lights in my life. From my earliest days, she conveyed a love and a confidence that I could do anything. My mother dazzled me in so many ways. And "dazzle" is the right word. She was stunningly beautiful and a talented concert pianist. She was a champion golfer and songwriter, and even wrote a campaign song for General Eisenhower in his victorious 1952 Presidential campaign ("Get Out And Fight For Ike.") She was active in community affairs, as Director of the YWCA in Pottsville and Chairman of the Women's Division of the Red Cross. My two best friends told me later how much they admired and appreciated my mother. She "was a gentle and beautiful woman . . . so vivacious and outgoing . . . she was always doing things for us."

She brought joy to everyone around her. No one benefited from that joy as much as I did.

My mother grew up in a privileged background and a highly educated family in Ottawa, Illinois. She went on to study piano and music in New York and Chicago as well as dramatics, dance and voice. She met my father through his sister, Margaret, when both attended Rosemont College in Rosemont, Pennsylvania. She and my father were married in 1937, the year before I was born.

Throughout my life, even as I was growing up, I appreciated that my mother would do anything to help ensure my future. I'm sure, for example, it was primarily her decision that I should go away to Portsmouth Priory in Portsmouth, Rhode Island, during my final two years of high school. No small part of the reason for that, I'm sure, was to *escape* the turmoil in our household.

The small role I play in the story my mother tells in this haunting book signals her desire to keep me removed from the challenge at home even though doing so was a personal sacrifice in her own life.

My sister Elizabeth was two years younger than I. We were very close growing up. Elizabeth was a beautiful girl. Many likened her looks to Grace Kelly. She was intelligent, enthusiastic, invariably one of the most popular girls in her class, kind and generous, altogether a wonderful young lady. She was a superb hockey player and that, sadly, led to the accident which controlled and contaminated the rest of her life. In high school, she incurred a freak hockey injury to her knee. It was devastating. The first operation on her knee was botched; so were the second or third. They occurred over the course of several years. Eventually, her knee became immobilized and had to be fused. Her doctors put her on pain-controlling drugs. She became addicted to them when she was in her late teens and early 20s.

I observed all this while I was going through college and then the Navy and beginning my career at P&G. I worried throughout that I was not doing all I should to help her. I think, in terms of linking her up with potential boyfriends, my shyness and the fact that I had very male friends got in the way. She came to Cincinnati to live with me for a while when I was dating my future wife, Francie. She had a job for a bit of time, but for reasons I can't recall, it didn't work out. She was unhappy in Cincinnati. I know I felt her presence might be getting in the way of developing my relationship with Francie, and I think she worried about that. I know I felt guilty about my feeling and do to this very day.

Elizabeth returned home to Philadelphia, to live with my mother. In 1972, she passed away due to an overdose of drugs.

This book brings home with agonizing clarity how hard my mother worked to try to help Elizabeth recover from her addiction and how hard it was to do it.

My mother writes about the "absence of justice." I've lived long enough to see the truth of that many times. It was certainly true of my sister's life. The freak hockey accident, the botched operations, the fused leg, led her to question her attractiveness. The constant pain led to the doctor's recommendation that she take medication to overcome that pain, and her own frustration at her "weak folly," as my mother put it, in becoming addicted to those drugs. My mother wonders in the book if any of us could have overcome such a similar challenge. So do I.

As my mother's story concludes, I was deeply moved by her brave and ever-so-honest confrontation about what faced her "in the present and what had bogged (her) down for many years before." She was being caught within the imprisonment of Elizabeth's affliction as she had been caught before by my father's alcoholism. Yet, as you have read, she never gave up. She wouldn't. I knew that, knowing her.

I recently read a very compelling book, *Mercy Justice*, by Bryan Stevenson, in which the author examines the source of the motivation he has brought to securing justice for men and women convicted of crimes and sentenced to lifetime imprisonment without parole. Stevenson writes that he had come to realize for the first time that his own life "was just full of brokenness."

In reading this, I was brought back to the recognition that I have my own "brokenness." "Brokenness" in looking back and wondering if I could have done more to support my sister and my mother at the most challenging times of their lives.

I have fought hard not to allow myself to be unduly depressed by this worry, concentrating rather on doing what I can for others today. Still, I know I could have done more.

But of this I am sure. My mother (and father and sister, too) would be very proud of what I have accomplished and thrilled by my wonderful family. I know my mother would say, *this is what I worked for; this makes it all worthwhile.* Without question, she took every step she could for me and my sister, too. She sacrificed herself for us.

My mother writes at the end of the book: "The only weapon with which I could keep fighting had been hope, for without hope, I knew there was no chance for myself or for (Elizabeth). She needed to be nourished in order to get well, and I believe the nourishment for anyone's problems was love—love based on complete faith and trust, and the joy of being loved in return. The source of (Elizabeth's) strength to fight her problem had to be this. I was sure. But was I capable of providing enough (love) for her?"

My mother's brutal courage and honesty ring forth in that last question. Who knows? Of this I am sure. She gave it everything she had.

My sister lived to meet Francie and attend our wedding; also to meet our first son John.

My mother lived to know our three sons but, sadly, not our one daughter. She was born after my mother passed away.

My mother passed away in 1975. Fortunately, she had visited with us the prior Christmas in Rome. The trip meant a great deal to her, for it was a celebratory year in the Catholic Church. One of its features was the opening of the holy door of St. Peter's. It was understood that all who passed through that door would receive a plenary indulgence, i.e., the forgiveness of all their sins. That was something my mother had been looking forward to. She was in a wheelchair by then. She asked us to take her through the door twice, which we did. She wanted to be doubly sure the plenary indulgence occurred. This was the last chance my mother had to see our children. We had feared this would be the case. Her emphysema, brought on by years of smoking, could not be held back.

Francie and I returned to Philadelphia for her funeral. There were countless tributes to her courage and accomplishments. I was reminded, once again, that, if it had not been for her, I never would have had the education or, more importantly, the confidence that allowed me to have the life I have been fortunate to have. From the very beginning to the very end, my mother was my greatest supporter.

I hope she is up in Heaven, able to look down on what she made possible.

My father passed away after a long illness in 1979. I think the last years of his life were his happiest.

Truth be told, I never felt as close to my father as a son would want to be with his father. I do not blame him for this. It is just a fact. However, I do remember happy times together. I recall him winning a golf championship at the country club we belonged to and fishing with me at Wallops Island off the Virginia coast. I remember him consoling me when my first dog, Blitzen, was killed right in front of me outside our house. I was five or six. He came home from work that afternoon and he took me to a movie. I remember how grateful I was that he did that; how secure and supported it made me feel.

I'll never know the challenges and, perhaps, demons that afflicted my father's life which led to his alcoholism and all the unhappiness that flowed from it. I think I tried to help him when I was a teenager and when I was in my 20s about as much as I could. I don't think he would have wanted me to do any more. He cared about me deeply. He loved me; there was never any doubt about that.

In publishing this book, I express my never-ending gratitude and love to my mother; my love for my father and sister; and my hope that life after death is real and that I will re-join them in happiness in Heaven.

Irma Pepper—Circa 1962

Sister and brother—Elizabeth and John—Circa 1945

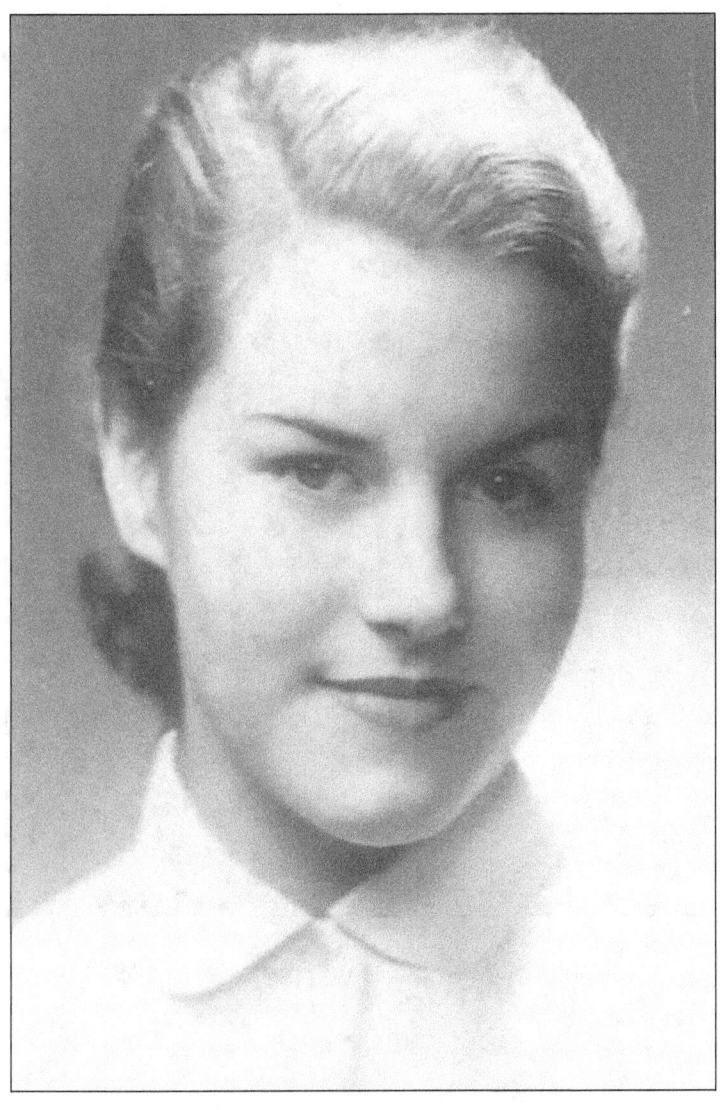

Elizabeth in her teenage years—Circa 1958

Elizabeth at her high school prom—Circa 1958

Elizabeth—Happy Times! Circa 1962

Graduation portrait—Circa 1962